All contents copyright © 2007 by Jennifer Seeley. All rights reserved.

No part of this document or the related files may be reproduced or transmitted in any form, by any means (electronic, photocopying, recording, or otherwise) without the prior written permission of the author.

Any **trademarks**, service marks, product names or named features in this book are assumed to be the property of their respective owners, and are used only for reference.

This guide is written to be helpful and practical and inform the reader, however nothing in this Guide is intended to replace common sense, legal, medical or other professional advice.

This book is dedicated to Wayne
For believing in me and encouraging me to write this book.

Table of Contents

Introduction..5

Terms/Definitions..................................8

My Story..11

What Brought you Here?......................................24

Helpful Insights 1..32

Two Transitions...36

Things to Ponder....................................39

Happiness Now!...45

The School of Observation
(Learning to walk, sit and act like a woman)...............49

Support...54

It is Time to Appreciate and Accept our Diversity!........60

Helpful Insights 2..63

Do not Worry about Why TOO Much......................65

Some Starting Steps for Feminizing your Look............68

Therapy..71

Helpful Insights 3..75

Dressing..77

Makeup………………………………………….....85

Skin Care……………………………………….....93

Hair…………………...………………………...98

Hair Removal……………...…………………….107

Hormones……………………………..………119

Picturing Yourself……………………….…..…...132

Voice……………………………………………134

Dating………………………….………….…...141

Safety…………………………………………….....151

Coming Out………………………………………156

Dealing with Criticism and Judgment from Others……..167

Your New Name……………………………….172

Helpful Insights 4………………………………....176

Facial Feminization Surgery (FFS)…………………178

Sex Reassignment Surgery (SRS or GRS)……………183

Helpful Insights 5………....………………………189

Suggested Order of Transitioning……………..….........192

Conclusion…………………...……………….....196

Introduction

Why did I write this book? I think a lot of transgendered women starting out do not know what to do. They may wonder, "What is a transition? What am I? Why do I feel this way?" I think many think a transition involves putting some makeup on and a dress and maybe getting a sex change operation (now called Sex Reassignment Surgery). These are all activities you may choose to do and can be a part of a transition, but there is really much more to it than that.

There is growth that has to happen inside of you. There are things you need to do to make your outside match your inside and to become what we call more "passable". You have to discover yourself and figure out who you are and what you want to do to be "you".

I started my transition 8 years ago, and am now living a healthy, happy life as a woman. I blend into society as a female, which I think is what many of us want to do (but not all, and that is ok too!). However, I had to figure a lot out for myself, especially at the beginning. I had no idea what to do. I had a rather ignorant picture of what to do as well. I just knew I wanted to be a woman and be myself finally. However, what to do?

When I started out, I gleaned information from different sources. I experimented and did a lot of learning as I went.

I have learned a lot in the past eight years. I have had a very positive transition, and am very happy with myself and feel like a well adjusted person. I lead a balanced life. I am very much at peace and happy with myself and my life. I look very nice and blend into society now.

Unfortunately, I have talked to many transgendered women over the years, who have not felt good about themselves. They are confused. Not sure what to do. They do not know how to make themselves presentable. They do not know what they are feeling, etc. They do not know who they really are many times. And some are doing things to their bodies they do not need to do, based on how they feel about themselves.

For the record, I did not start out feeling good about myself or having all these positive feelings I have now. I started out as a shy, insecure, self-critical and scared person. The transition brought me out of my shell and taught me a lot about myself and life. It can do the same for you, as long as you let it. It is a very empowering journey!

So, I decided to write this book for a few reasons:

1) To present a roadmap to follow on your transition, so you will know what you need to do. In essence, to give you a practical guide to follow on what to do, not a bunch of theory.
2) To provide some guidance in finding out who you are and what you want to do
3) To provide support when you are alone.
4) To provide helpful insights in order to give you a healthy balanced outlook on yourself and your transition. These insights are VERY important to understand.

Many of us really are alone when we start. We often do not have somebody to talk to. We have often lived our whole lives with this "secret" inside of us.

There are some books out there, but most of them are written from a psychological standpoint, by professionals. This is a book written by another transsexual that understands from experience what it is like to go through what you are going through. It is meant to be practical and helpful, not necessarily scientific.

I would like to make a quick note that this book is written for Male to Female Transgendered people rather than Female to Male. I did not feel I had enough experience or knowledge to write it for Female to Male as well, so I apologize.

As I stated previously, when I started out, I was alone. There was not a book to tell me what to do. Transitioning was somewhat confusing and overwhelming to me.

I also did not have anybody to talk to about my transition. I think a lot of "fledgling" transgendered women have the same issue.

Both the mental and physical aspects of your transition are covered in this book. The first half deals more with the mental/inside aspect of your transition (which is the most important) and the second half deals more with the physical/outside aspects of your transition. However, there is advice on both throughout the book.

I would recommend reading this book the entire way through the first time, and then going back later to the specific sections you need to review or understand more fully later as you go through a certain step or phase in your transition. I have tried to divide this book into easy to read chapters on very specific topics so that you can easily find a specific topic later that you need to reference.

This book will help you to have a healthy transition and emerge as the person you have always wanted to be!

Terms/Definitions

These are my own definitions of these terms as I learned them and interpret them. I am listing these for reference in this book only.

People have different names for different things, but for the purposes of this book when I talk about certain kinds of transgendered people, I will use these labels. No offense is meant by any of them. Everyone is special and appreciated. Remember, labels are just labels. They just make for ease of reference, but you may not fit one particular "label". You may be a combination or something entirely unique. There is no judgment here at all. Any use of the word "man" is not meant offensively. It strictly refers to being born genetically male. This does not mean you are a "man" if you do not feel like a man. Any use of the word "penis" as well is not meant offensively but strictly as a reference term for that part of the anatomy. Any use of the word "he" in this book is also just meant for reference. If I ever use it by accident in a way offensive to you as the reader, please forgive me. I am not calling you a man ever, if you do not feel like a man.

So here are my definitions for use in this book.

Transition – The process of transforming yourself from a male to a female or whomever you want to be – whether that be a full time or part time female. This process involves a variety of steps you can take which are described in this book.

Crossdresser (CD) – This is a man who simply likes to wear women's clothing. He may do it for fun or because it makes him feel good or peaceful or to attract men (if he is a gay man). He does not want to be a woman and may even like being a man. Many crossdressers are heterosexual even and happily married. He may be gay or straight

Transvestite (TV) – This is a man who is sexually aroused by women's clothing. It is more about sex. The clothing itself can actually bring sexual arousal. This tends to be more of a fetish.

Drag Queen (DQ) – This is sometimes referred to as a female impersonator as well. This is someone who dresses up to look like a woman, perhaps flamboyantly, or perhaps for shows. They may or may not have a desire to become a woman.

Transgendered (TG) – This is a catch all phrase for all types of transgendered people. Crossdressers, Transvestites, Drag Queens, Transsexuals, Intersexed People.

Intersexed (Hermaphrodite) – These people were born with both male and female genitalia.

Transsexual (TS or Tgirl) – This is a woman "born in a man's body". This is a genetic male who truly identifies inside as a woman. A TS feels she truly is a woman. She wants to be a woman, in whatever capacity she chooses.

Shemale – This is a person who wants to appear and live as a woman but enjoys her male side and playing the "male role" sexually.

Sex Reassignment Surgery (SRS) – This is surgery whereby a person's body is changed in the genital area to resemble the opposite gender's. The penis is essentially inverted and a vagina created (of course it is much more complicated than that).

Gender Reassignment Surgery (GRS) – This is the same as SRS.

Passable – This refers to appearing as a genetic female to the world, as much as possible. In other words, you "pass" other people's gazes so they do not realize you are a TS.

Full Time – This refers to changing the gender you are living in and living that way all the time, or "full time". In other words, you would live your life full time as a female.

Hormone Therapy (HT) – This is where a person takes estrogen (and sometimes progesterone and a testosterone blocker as well) to help to feminize their bodies and appearance. The hormones can be taken through injection, orally through a pill, or with a patch on the skin (which is the best and safest method, in my opinion).

Pre-Operative – A transsexual woman who has not had SRS yet, but plans on it.

Post-operative – A transsexual woman who has had SRS.

Non-Operative – A transsexual woman who plans to stay pre-operative.

MTF – This is a Male to Female Transsexual.

Harry Benjamin Standards of Care – These are the rules followed by therapists and doctors for transsexuals seeking hormone therapy or SRS.

My Story

I will share my story here simply because I know it is always helpful to hear other transgendered people's stories. There are oftentimes many things in other girls' stories we can relate to and it feels good to know somebody else felt like we did or experienced something we did. Also, hearing my story and how I overcame my trials and tribulations to happily become who I wanted to be will hopefully inspire you to realize YOU can do the same!

Just realize this was my own personal story. Everyone's is different, which is part of what makes us all our unique and wonderful selves!

I was always a rather feminine person, especially as a younger child. I did not have any inhibitions about that yet, and so I just acted how I acted. I had the innocence of youth, which is a wonderful thing!

I was what would be considered a "sissy" I suppose. I always loved doing girl things and would hang out with girls and play girl games, but never really wanted to hang out with other boys.

However, I remember feeling like something was just not "quite right" as a young child in early grade school. I wanted to be a girl, but my thinking was not that sophisticated at that age to put what I was feeling into words or know what it was I was feeling. I also did not know there was anything "wrong" with me for feeling that way. (And there was nothing wrong with me!)

So I just happily went along, being a normal child. My best friend was Cheryl, the girl who lived next door. Looking back, we were pretty much best girlfriends. We really had fun together. However, my Mom wanted me to play with boys. This is when the shame spiral started and I started to be made to feel "bad" about who I was. My Mom started to pressure me to play with the boys on the block. They did not like me. They made fun of me because I was not athletic. I did not WANT to play football or other sports, and I did not know why.

My Mom started enrolling me in every sport she could. This was around third grade. I remember her sticking me in Boy Scouts, gymnastics, basketball, touch football, and swimming. Not to mention sports camps. I hated all of them except swimming. But I went. I learned to do things that scared me or bothered me, so it was a strengthening experience.

I realize my Mom was just trying to get me interested in what boys "should" be interested in and to make me well rounded.

However, my heart was still in doing girl things. I was not a doll person or anything like that (even at that age, I kind of thought dolls looked a little creepy, like they would come to life and murder me in my sleep!) However, I still loved playing with other girls and such, just like any other little girl would do, frankly, at that age.

I still played with Cheryl next door and my Mom got more and more disgusted. I remember her coming home from work and I would be playing next door with Cheryl in their backyard, and my Mom just shaking her head and looking disgusted and I would get a knot in my stomach because she was mad at me. This was at like 9 or 10. I really started feeling bad about myself.

Then I started to want to put makeup on. I swear I have NO idea what compelled me. I still say I was too young to even think this out. So I would sneak in the bathroom and play with makeup a bit and then wash it off.

Well one day I did not wash some eye shadow all the way off and one of my older sisters asked, "Is that eye shadow?" Well, she told Mom and Mom and Dad sat me down on the living room couch and gave me a good stern talking to and told me boys do not do that and they were not pleased. I was humiliated.

That is when I learned to hide things.

As puberty hit, and I started to develop hair in new places, for some reason I started wanting to shave it. Once again, I am not sure why. It was like something inside of me just knew I was female and wanted to match that up. So I would shave sometimes in the bath tub. I also started sitting down to go to the bathroom a lot, and would tuck myself under while I was in there.

As puberty hit, so did my attraction to boys. Now I realize, not every TS is attracted to men but I was. However, being raised in a strict Christian church, I was told homosexuality was practically worse than murder. This also began to confuse me about my gender "issue" I had been having. Because of how I was feeling, I assumed that every gay man or boy wanted to be a girl. That was how I felt. It made logical sense to me. I realize now, that is not true.

However, one night I was over at my brother's apartment and I was reading a magazine while my parents and he talked, and there was an article about a woman who had been born a man but had Sex Reassignment Surgery (of course, back then, they called it a Sex Change) and was now married. The article was more about some issue with the marriage, but what got to me was what she had done, which was to have this "Sex Change". I had never heard of such a thing! It also talked about how she had felt and how she truly had always wanted to be a woman and felt like a woman inside, and now she was one. And I thought, wow that is me! That would TOTALLY solve my problem.

Just realize, up until then I did not realize anybody else felt the way I did. That is one reason I could not even label myself. That story really stuck in my head though as it told me there was something I could do to "fix" myself and there was a "way out" of feeling bad.

Then sometime later, I was watching a movie on television, and this very feminine gay man in the movie said, he felt like a "woman trapped in a man's body". That may be a more common phrase today (or not), but I had never heard it and I completely identified with it. It described me to a tee. I finally had words to describe how I felt inside. Unfortunately, I could not tell anybody these words, not even my parents, which is what we transsexuals do. We go through this struggle all on our own usually, with nobody to trust enough to tell.

I started to get made fun of more in 6th grade for how I acted. And I did not know how to change. I remember an entire science class making fun of me and the nicest girl in school finally made fun of me and it just broke my heart. "Why didn't anybody like me?" I agonizingly wondered. I felt totally unlovable and alone. I went to my next class, felt a cry welling up, and just walked out of the class and went to the bathroom and cried.

Kids fortunately, are adaptable. So, since my voice got made fun of and the way I walked and everything got made fun of, I became shy. It was kind of like a self defense mechanism, looking back. If I did not open my mouth, nobody could make fun of how I talked. I also learned to just keep to myself. If I kept to myself, I did not get made fun of so much.

Of course, I was not the only unpopular kid. I think all kids suffer that to some degree. I just had it to a higher degree being what I was. And kids were not so open-minded back then as they are today.

I became a reader. I loved to read, and still do. I could go in my bedroom or sit in the middle of school at lunch break (nobody would let me sit by them – literally) and read. That really helped me. I could escape into books. I became more self sufficient. I learned to be ok not having a bunch of friends and with everybody not liking me (although it still hurt me). That lesson helped me later in life.

At home, I was still having a few problems. My mother one day mocked the way I talked. She told me I sounded "like a big sissy." She mocked the way I moved my arms. My mother was not always the nicest person, although really she was a good mother most of the time. It was just a different time. For the record, she was also a very nice person most of the time. As I said, it was a different time. Parents cannot help but want us to conform to their image and dreams for us. They should love and accept us just how we are, but parents are human too, and do not always do that. That is all that was going on. It hurt, but I know it was not done out of mean intentions. I think she was also trying to prevent me from getting made fun of.

Anyway, Mom told me to start lowering my voice, to speak in more monotone voice. She told me to not move my arms when I talked. Basically, lose my personality. So I did, for the most part, although I never could really hide it completely.

I learned to walk more "masculine". I wore suits. How miserable! This is when people started talking to me like I was a masculine man. Trying to make me into that, what they wanted me to be. And I was never exactly butch, but I learned to act how I was expected to, at least to a certain degree.

I was miserable inside, but I was learning to cope with that. It is very hurtful and psychologically damaging for everybody to be treating you like something you are not. It is like you want to scream, "No! That's not me! THIS is what I am. Why don't you like THAT?" To me, this was the most hurtful and psychologically damaging part of my pre-transition years. People not relating to me as I wanted to be related to, as the person I wanted to be, not the person THEY wanted me to be.

And through all this, there was the religious issue. I felt like I was going to go to hell. Especially as I thought wanting to be a woman made me gay (which it does not, but I did not understand that then – not that there is anything wrong with being gay either for the record). So I was trying to suppress my feelings as much as I could.

However, since I was religious back then I would also pray to God (no offense is meant here to anybody in regards to religion. I am simply relating my feelings at the time). Every night I would pray, "Please just take this feeling away from me or make me a woman overnight. Let me wake up as a woman or without this feeling anymore. Please, please, please." I was miserable. I hated myself. I thought, "This is my life? I have to be miserable my whole life and go to hell? Other people do not have to deal with this. Why do I?"

And my prayers were never answered – at least at that time it seemed they were not. However, my prayers were answered, just in a different way, and it took awhile. I do believe there is a guiding hand in our lives (religious or not), and I want to show you how there was in my life so you will know there is one in yours as well.

College time. I went to Purdue University, and all of a sudden nobody knew me and I started to come out of my shell. I became more outgoing again. People were a little more accepting. I became an Electrical Engineer. I got a job down in SC and moved to Augusta, Georgia. I concentrated on my career. I did not do a thing about my sexuality or my transsexuality. I just kept to myself, went to work, made a few friends, and basically ignored who I was as best I could.

When I was about 27, my Dad was diagnosed with lung cancer. So I wanted to move back up north. I found a job about 100 miles from my parents back up north and moved. I was a plant engineer and a maintenance manager of a Union Plant. What a miserable experience. There was a lot of back stabbing. I worked for a horribly mean woman. The Union people seemed to be constantly filing grievances and trying to take advantage of me. I was still shy and trying to be nice to everybody. It was the worst job for me. They definitely needed a hard-assed man and that was not me!

So 6 months later I got fired from my job. The day after that, the lady who was buying my condominium down south backed out. So I had two mortgages (I had bought a house up north), no job and no prospects. So I ended up moving back with my parents to help with Dad, and get my life back on track. Boy, was I humiliated, though.

I tried to start up a business selling phone cards as I did not want to trust my future to anybody else ever again. I lost almost $6000 of my savings. I thought maybe computers would be the way to go. This was back in the late 1990's, and there seemed to be computer jobs aplenty, and I figured I could take better control of my career that way, learning whatever skills I needed to.

I found a local school in the North suburbs of Chicago to learn Oracle (computers). I went for 7 months and worked hard. I had to drive 45 miles each way. But I was determined to do something where I could have more control of my future.

I finally sold my condo at a LOSS of $4000 from what I paid for it. I sold my house up north with a rent to own. The lady who bought it bounced two checks on me, but I made it.

Somehow I managed to avoid bankruptcy. I learned to play with my bills. Bounce things around. I learned I would not die if I did not pay something exactly on time.

All the time as all this stuff is happening, I am thinking, "Why does God hate me so much? What did I do to deserve this?"

My mother tells me I am depressing her because I am looking worried, which made me feel guilty. So I learned to hide that. I was all about hiding things, obviously.

But I am determined to turn my life around. I got through that school and I got a great job with a little consulting firm downtown.

Why am I telling you all this? Well, I learned a lot from that experience. Mainly, I learned that I am tough. I am resourceful. I can get through things. I am not weak – I am strong. That goes for my experiences as a child too. I learned how to handle not being liked by everybody. I did not expect to be popular. I learned to be strong. To handle being alone. I learned to live on the edge and not be safe all the time (because I HAD to). These are all great skills for transitioning.

Not to mention, those little prayers I had been putting out to the Universe as a child were being answered in a very strange way without me realizing it.

My Dad passed away about 6 months after I got my first computer job. I was 28. I marched on with my computer job, bought a nice townhome in the Chicago suburbs, and also finally began to explore who I was - at least my sexuality.

I figured, well if I become a woman, that will just devastate everybody, so maybe I can live as a gay man. That is more "socially acceptable" at this point (although of course not totally) and they could handle that easier.

So I tried that. However, it never fit for me, and I did not quite totally understand why.

The thing was, I wanted these guys to treat me like the "girl". Well they did not want that. They wanted a man, which of course, is perfectly understandable, since they are gay! I was definitely not prime dating material to gay men, and when I did date, I always had to pretend. I was not happy.

So I pretty much kept to myself again.

Unfortunately, I was still agonizing inside about how I felt.

I was still dealing with religious issues. I was pretty much disenchanted with the church and their judgmental ways (I realize there are open churches now). I was becoming angrier and angrier with God. I remember thinking, "Why did you even bring me here? I cannot change. I'm just a big joke to You, aren't I God? You brought me here with NO chance to ever go to heaven so why did you bring me here? I'm doomed to hell. I may as well do what I want."

For the record, my views on all this stuff have totally changed. I am a Spiritual person now and have a very positive image of God and the Universe. I just do not go to church myself. Organized religion is not for me, at least at this time, but I am Spiritual. I realize for other people organized religion is a good thing, and that is fine too. If you go to a supportive church (whatever you religion you are) and enjoy that, then I say, keep on going. That is just fine. You do what is right for you, whether that is going to church or NOT going to church. If you do go, just make sure you go someplace that is supportive of whom you are.

But I am not here to preach. That is all a very personal issue for everybody. I am just relating my own experience as I went through my transition.

My Mom was diagnosed with leukemia about a year after my Dad died. She was in the hospital for 1-2 months at a time with chemotherapy. I was working in downtown Chicago, so I would walk a half hour each way to see her each day, wash her clothes, take care of her house and bills. I was very co-dependent still (not that I should not have helped my mom, I was happy to. She did a lot of good too). Well one day I am sitting in the room and all she can talk about is my brother calling every day from Texas. Never a thank you to me. IN fact, everybody just seemed to always take me for granted, no matter how much I went out of my way or did.

And the resentment inside me was building.

Then, all of a sudden, it clicked.

The moment that changed my life.

I do not know why it happened, but it literally happened in an instant. All of a sudden I GOT IT. It was a Saturday morning and I was sitting there listening to my mother talk about how wonderful my siblings were and not a thank you to me ever (although I know she appreciated me), and I thought, "I am living my life for everybody else and resenting them for it, and it is my choice to do that. It is my choice to not risk being different and getting criticized and live my life as I want. Do I want to wake up when I am 60 or lying on my death bed and regret not living my life? Not being who I am? This is just who I AM. It is not something I am DOING. I am about to lose my second parent. Life is precious. I better live it!"

And so my formal transition began at that point. I was 32.

I say formal transition, because I really feel like I was transitioning my whole life. Those first 32 years, I was finding myself. Finding what I wanted. Becoming ok with who I was.

That is one of those wonderful things that starts to happen at around age 30. You start to realize it is ok to be different. You start having more confidence in yourself. You start knowing more what you want in life as you have gotten out there in the world and lived some.

My transition started at exactly the right time. I was ready now. Yours started at exactly the right time too, no matter what your age. Look what happened with me. I wanted it when I was much younger, obviously. And I thought my prayers were not being answered. However, I would not have been able to handle it at that younger age (although some can). I just was not sure enough of myself and strong enough to just be myself at that age. Plus, I did not really understand yet that this was WHO I was. I had to live a little to learn that lesson. Not to mention all the career problems I had led me to a career that was much more supportive of my transition. So there really was a guiding hand of some kind in my life, as I believe there is in everybody's (this is not meant in an offensive or religious way at all). Just trust that you were guided to where you are now, and you are exactly where you are supposed to be. Your transition is happening at exactly the right time, and at just the right pace.

Back to my transition.

I started off very slowly. I found a store online that catered to crossdressers. There are several of these online. So I bought some clothes and a wig. I read on the internet what I could. I found a couple chat rooms and chatted with some girls, but I was having trouble relating to them. They seemed to be all about clothes and the sexual side, and I was feeling like I was screwed up or a misfit somehow.

There really was not any good practical resource. Which is one reason I am writing this book.

I started electrolysis and laser to remove hair about 6 months later. I looked for over a year and a half and found a great therapist in my area. Then I started on hormones. I went full time. I legally changed my name. I was on a roll, marching towards Sex Reassignment Surgery. (Note, I will relate more about my transition experiences throughout this book.)

Then 7 months after I went on hormones, I developed horrible pains in my chest that bent me over and kept me awake all night. Long story short, I had blood clots in both lungs (pulmonary embolism). So I sat in the hospital hooked up to an IV for 8 days and started wondering, what does this mean? Does this mean I am done with my transition?

At the end of that episode, though, I had a wonderful healthy new perspective on my transition and on my life. I had taken my health for granted for one thing. I had let a doctor and a transition control my health. I had transitioned with total disregard for my health. That is not good. Good health and a successful transition can go together.

I began to eat right. I began to read a lot about health and nutrition.

I realized that a drug did not make me a woman, no matter what the TG community or men or society says. I WAS a woman already.

But I was still going to get SRS. Then I went to get my second therapist's letter. She really grilled me about not being on hormones. I stayed calm throughout all her questions, but finally I said, "Look, I ended up in the hospital from them, I just don't want to risk my health. I personally do not feel I need them to be a woman." Then she mentioned some concern about my health after SRS since the body needs hormones and I would be removing my main source of hormones, even if it was not my chosen hormone.

Then I heard a couple stories of girls dying during SRS due to a blood clot going to their brain.

This is not meant as a cautionary tale to not get SRS. That is a personal choice. I am just discussing what I went through.

In any case, I thought, "You know, I am healthy. I am well adjusted. I am living my life as who I want to be and being treated as who I want. Why risk my health and happiness?" So I decided to not go through with the SRS.

That was my personal choice. It may not be yours. And that is ok. Everyone has their own personal preferences.

But I can tell you I am completely treated as a woman now. I am very happy. I have a great husband (although he and I have really had our challenges, as any couple does). I think I have a healthy philosophy about transitioning and how to do it in a healthy, positive, successful way.

I will share what I have learned and hopefully give you a lot of helpful insights and practical advice on transitioning in this book.

This book will not try to discourage you from doing anything. Everything is a personal choice. The only thing I will detract you from doing is something that will risk your health. You can still go on hormones and have SRS if you choose. But I want you to do it in a safe, healthy, informed way. Along with all the other things a transition entails.

What Brought you Here?

What brought you here? What made you buy this book?

I think we all have our own personal journey in life, our own inner desires and inner "compulsions". That inner voice is telling you something. It wants to be heard. That inner voice may have brought you to this book to learn more about yourself and what you can do.

As you read this book, it is important to realize that you are a unique person. It is ok to be different, even within the transgendered community. Variety is a wonderful thing. So as you read this, put aside all judgment, of yourself and others. Nobody is better or worse than anybody else. We may be different in our desires and who we are, but we are all special, and we all want to let a part of us that is hidden inside out.

Below are some different "categories" of transgendered people that you may identify with. All of these are OK. There is no one "legitimate" way to be.

1) Some just love the look and feel of women's clothing. It makes them feel good, peaceful, happy, whatever. However, they do not desire to live as a woman. These are usually called crossdressers.
2) Some wear the clothes to attract men. It is purely for sexual reasons. However, they do not really want to be a woman other than to attract men.
3) Some get sexually aroused by women's clothing. These are typically called transvestites.
4) Some love the attention. They just find it fun to dress up and go out.
5) Some are entertainers. They love to dress up as a female (often very convincingly) and sing or dance on stage or

       impersonate celebrities or just women in general. These are sometimes called drag queens or female impersonators.
6) Some feel like they are a woman trapped in a man's body. They have always felt like a girl, thought like girl, wanted to BE a girl, but they were born in a man's body and have had to live like that. At some point in their life, they just finally feel compelled to let their "real self" out.

Take a look at these categories. Where do you think you fit in? This can change. You are not locked into anything. This is simply a starting point. Maybe you are combination of two of the categories. The one thing that is important is to see for now is if you fit more in the first 5 categories, as this will prevent you from doing something major to your body you might not be able to undo later.

It is ok whatever you are. You just do not want to pay a bunch of money for surgeries or go on hormones or get surgeries or get hair removed, and get all caught up in that and then wonder a few years down the road, what have I done. There is so much you can still do and not do anything that you will regret later. Your "category" may change later, which is ok too.

You do not have to transition to get men or dress or get attention. You can dress and get attention without doing anything serious, transition wise. You do not have to go through a whole transition if you simply enjoy dressing and looking like a woman sometimes.

So if you are not sure of what you are right now or what you want to do, just take it slowly. You will find yourself on this journey. You may think you just want to dress and discover you really do want to be a woman. Or you may start out thinking you want to be a woman, but are happy just dressing sometimes.

We suppress these things and then they come to the surface once we start letting our guard down. We may be confused when we start our transition and are not sure what we are and find that out on the journey. We have had to pretend to be what others want for so long we may have even forgotten who we are, and have to rediscover that in our transition.

As I said, just be careful to not do anything drastic until you are sure. You can always dress and go out and explore and be you if you are not sure yet.

Now if you are in category 6, you are probably becoming more and more uncomfortable in your own skin. You have given up yourself for so long and it is really starting to wear on you. You might feel like a fake. You might resent people for not letting you be you.

The "real" you is getting more and more restless inside, no longer content to be ignored or suppressed. The real you is just getting stronger and more restless, no longer content to only be on the inside. It is a little like the alien in the first "Alien" movie. You just feel like it is gonna burst out! Only not that gross (whew). And it is beautiful, not ugly. But other then that, it is a great analogy!

You feel positively COMPELLED to do something, anything. This is probably true no matter which category you are in, but especially in category 6 (a TS).

Life is too short to not live it. Remember, **only you have to live your life**. Nobody else does. People may not like what you are doing, but they are not having to live in your skin. YOU are.

You are not helping anybody by being miserable. You will only end up resenting them. And do you want to wake up when you are 60 or 70 or 80 and wonder, why didn't I live my life?

And if you are older, that is ok. Whenever you arrive at this point is ok. The world is more open now than it used to be, so it was harder earlier in your life if you are older. You still have life to live, and can do this for yourself now.

No matter what your age, love yourself enough to do SOMETHING, even if it is just accept yourself. You can do as little or as much as you want.

Throughout this process, some fear (or a lot of fear) is normal. That is ok. Be gentle with yourself. Push yourself a little, but do not let anybody else push you. Take little baby steps at first. You will find the more you push a little, the easier it gets. The fear starts to melt away. "Stepping out of your comfort zone" becomes a habit and ends up not being as uncomfortable any more (ironically enough!).

You also do not have to decide how far you want to go yet. The answer to that question will come to you as you go along. When I started my transition, I still was not sure if I would have the guts to go very far, so I just simply started to dress some at home and put on makeup and do some reading online. However, once I started, the floodgates opened inside of me and my true female self just had to come out all the way and a year and a half later I was full time. However, I did not know that I would be that brave when I made up my mind to start my transition. So just decide to do SOMETHING now, however small. You can go as far or not far as you want. You can even change your mind and go right back to how you are now if you find that is a happier place for you.

The first thing to do as you start your transition is to let go of all judgment of yourself. You are ok. In fact, you are wonderful! You were made this way for a wonderful reason. You are not a bad person. You are not selfish. You are not wrong. It is not wrong to feel a certain way. It is not wrong to just "be".

We are all unique. The problem is, we are trained to blend in, follow the crowd, and make everybody ELSE happy.

Unfortunately, in the process, we lose our true selves. Really, the transsexual journey is every human being's journey. Most people suppress their true self through childhood and lose it. TS women do not dress or express their desire to be a girl or act like they want because their parents or society told them that was "bad." However other people make other compromises too. They do not do what they want because it is nor practical or what their dad did. They do not live where they want because their family wants them close. Etc.

We all have these issues. It is ok. It is part of life. You lose a part of yourself, then you find it and reawaken it.

You need to find your true self, nurture it, rescue it, and bring it out with love.

As I said, everybody, transsexual or not, has parts of themselves that they have forgotten or lost or suppressed. You are lucky, believe it or not, because you are finding your true self and learning to bring it out!

This will also probably translate into other areas. You may make career changes, location changes, whatever it is that you have always wanted to do. If you do this, you can do anything!

However, that is beyond the scope of this book. We will cover specifically bringing out your true gender self – whether that be a feminine male, full time female, part time female, or whatever you want to be.

Whatever it is, you are special. There is only one you. You really can not be like anybody else, no matter how much you try. So love yourself. Embrace yourself. You are awesome!

Stop looking at being different as being a curse. Look at it as a gift. It is what makes you, you. Think of your uniqueness as an asset. Everybody can blend in. Not everybody can be unique, or has the courage to be unique at least.

This is a unique and exciting experience you are having. How many people get to live both genders? How many people get the chance to truly find themselves? How many people get the chance to stand out?

There is a key lesson I learned in my transition that you will want to remember as you go on this journey: People react to us the way that we think of ourselves.

So if you are comfortable with who you are, they will be comfortable with who you are. If you are ok with you, they will be ok with you. Trust me, it works. And if they are not ok, you will not even notice it. Your field of vision will change so you do not attract those people into your life or you won't notice if they're not open to you.

If you are UNCOMFORTABLE with yourself or something about you, they will be too. And we all have things we're uncomfortable with. When something comes up, just be gentle with yourself. It kind of tells you something you are not comfortable with and then you can work on that.

Let me give you an example of this from my own experience. For me, my voice was my challenge and what bothered me most. I was so self conscious about my voice. I hated my voice. I figured it gave me away. Everytime somebody called me "Sir" (even by accident), I would be so embarrassed. So guess what, I kept getting experiences to confirm that my voice was awful. Even though my friends and family told me it was fine, that I had a very feminine voice. Nope, I was not going to believe them.

It got so bad that within 2 days in my business, I had two nasty incidents. IN the first, a man wrote me an email stating that I was not fooling anybody and that I was obviously a man. In the second, I was asked incredulously if I was a man or a woman by another customer. Talk about humiliating!

Well, that woke me up. I knew I had done something to attract that. SO I started listening to my voice. I liked it. It really was a pretty voice. It was NOT a man's voice. It was not exactly female (although close), but it was definitely not male. It was a TS voice. Well, I am a TS, am I not? Am I ashamed of that? No! Why should I be? So, I decided to fall in love with my voice. I became very comfortable with it. I stopped trying to mask it. So guess what? It sounded less fake. I was very comfortable with it. And guess what else? Nobody has given me a hard time for my voice since. And I do not remember the last time I got called Sir.

Just an example. See how a shift in my own thinking, changed how the world reacted to me? You can do the same thing! And do not beat up on yourself for not liking something about yourself. It is part of the process.

There is a sentence I read once that I think is so important to remember. "Treating myself like a precious object will make me strong."

Write that down and post it somewhere or carry it with you to remind you. Start treating yourself better! Stop beating up on yourself! Treat yourself like you would your own child. Loving, forgiving, gently.

No, you do not have to turn selfish or completely self centered. But you do have to learn to love yourself too. You do have to stop thinking your wants make you bad. This really is just who you ARE, not something you are doing. Is a man bad for building his muscle to be who he wants to be or a woman for having plastic surgery or makeup to look how she wants? Of course not. Or anybody pursuing what they want. You are just trying to be who you are.

That is part of the magic of being human. We can be whatever we want. Something puts these desires inside us, and I believe these desires are our true selves wanting to express. It is what we were put here for. And I think if we have a continuing desire, it is telling us something. And I think it is proof that we can do it.

So let us get started on the journey.

One point. The nice thing about this journey is you do not have to take every turn. Just do what you want. Do what is right for you. Only you know your situation. Only you know what you want. If you are not sure you want to do something, by all means do NOT do it. That is telling you something.

However, as I stated previously, do push yourself a little if you want something. Getting uncomfortable is the only way you will grow. And it is worth it.

Helpful Insights 1

Throughout this book, I will include these short little "nuggets" that you should understand to have a good healthy outlook on your transition, yourself, and your life. These are concepts I learned throughout my transition that really helped me have a very healthy and positive transition, and will help you do the same.

Here are the first "key concepts".

> **1) There is never a perfect time to start your transition.**

It is along the lines of, "there is never a perfect time to have a baby" or "there is never a perfect time to get married." In other words, do not keep putting off doing anything waiting for the perfect time when you will have enough money, be in the perfect situation to transition, be in the perfect job, have all your ducks in a row, etc. If you do keep waiting for the "perfect time" you will constantly be postponing doing anything, and then you will NEVER get started. Life is precious. Do not miss out on it! You deserve to do something! Even if it is small! Remember, you do not have to go all or nothing. You can at least see a therapist or dress or do something small to get started.

> **2) Enjoy the journey!**

Do not be impatient for the ending, whether that is going full time or SRS or just going out dressed the first time. Enjoy the journey. This is a unique experience. Enjoy! You only get to do this life once, so enjoy it. Enjoy each step. You do not want to get to the end of your transition, and then wonder, now what? You will be setting yourself up for a letdown if your final destination (e.g. SRS, living full time, dressing, whatever) is your only goal and what you think you need to be happy.

3) **Your transition is a journey of acceptance.**

Not just about being a woman, but also accepting who you are, your differences, your uniqueness, your specialness. Learning to accept yourself is one of the greatest feelings in the world and one of the best things you can do for your happiness and peace of mind.

4) **Have balance in your life.**

We all get somewhat obsessed with our transition for awhile. It is normal at the beginning to be that way. It is exciting. We are finally becoming who we are. We have that sense of adventure and peace and we cannot help but pursue it wholeheartedly.

However, just be careful (especially if you are younger and have not started a career or other things) that you pursue ALL areas of your life – career, relationships, hobbies, friendships. You do not want to just be about your transsexuality. In other words, being a TS is part of who you are, but it does not define you anymore than a woman is solely defined by being a woman or a man by being a man. You do not want to focus ALL your energy on your transition and not have a career you want, hobbies you want. These are precious years. You want to experience all of them, not just your transition. And balance is important. These other areas help us through the down periods in our transition.

5) **Do not feel inferior to genetic women.**

You are not inferior to them. You are simply a different kind of woman. There are manly looking genetic females, ugly women, tall women, women with big noses, etc, as well as beautiful women, fit women, modelesque women, etc. You are not inferior because you are different. You are a special woman too.

6) **Do not compare yourself to other transsexuals or other women in general.**

Have you ever compared yourself to somebody? Do you ever come out feeling better? Probably not. Plus, we tend to compare in one little area. If you have to compare, compare yourself in all areas. Maybe they look what you deem better, but you have more self acceptance and are happier. Or maybe they have a better relationship you deem, but you have a lot of great friends and they do not.

Realize also that genetic women deal with the same insecurities. They compare themselves to other women, and feel inferior to models on the covers of magazines just like you. Comparing does not work for them either!

We are all different. You cannot be exactly like anybody else. Each Transsexual's journey is personal and her own, and what is right for another, may or may not be right for you. So do not compare yourself to others. You just follow your own journey and do what is right for you and what you want to do.

7) **Push yourself a bit, but do not allow anybody else to push you.**

Transitioning (in whatever form that takes for you) can be scary or uncomfortable at times. As human beings, we naturally try to avoid feeling scared or uncomfortable or in pain. Sometimes, we have to push ourselves past that to get to the next level and ultimately live a happier life as ourselves, which may involve some pain and discomfort in the process.

However, other people (family, friends, other TG's, etc) with their own opinions and agenda may try to get you to follow the path they would choose for you or the path they think you should take. You do what YOU think is right. What is right for YOU. Only you have to live your life. They do not. So be strong enough to stand up for yourself and not be pushed into doing something you are not ready for or are not sure is right for you or be talked out of doing something that you have decided is right for you.

Two Transitions

As we go through this transformation, it is important to realize that there are really two transitions we go through.

The first transition is INTERNAL.

This is actually the most important part of the transition. This involves figuring out what you want (remember this can always change, and that is ok), who you are, what you want to do, how far you want to go in your transition, how you want to live, what changes you want to or are willing to make in your life, etc. Even more importantly, this internal transition involves becoming comfortable and accepting of who you are.

You have actually been going through this internal transition since you had your first yearning about this, perhaps as a child. Struggling on the inside. Fighting your feelings perhaps. Denying your feelings even. Trying to figure out who you are. What you want to do. Learning to accept yourself. Learning to love who you are. Developing courage to start doing something about your desires.

You have been learning to let that inner person come out –whether that is just a more feminine man, a full time woman, a crossdresser, or a part time woman - whatever it is that is right for you.

You want to become ok with who you are. Comfortable with yourself. Confident in yourself.

This does not happen overnight. We as transgendered people have typically suppressed who we are and lived our lives to please others to the point where we either feel guilty for doing something for ourselves or being ourselves, or sometimes we do not even

KNOW who we are or what we want because we were always being what other people told us to be.

This internal transition is the key. Once you are ok with who you are and know what you want to be and do, the second transition will follow very naturally. You will know what you want to do and what is right for you and you will just kind of be "pulled" to the right steps in the second transition. So concentrate more on this internal transition, especially at first.

So what is this second transition?

The second transition is the EXTERNAL transition.

This is what most people think of. This involves making your outer appearance match your inner self. This is an exciting and intimidating experience for all.

Sooner or later in your internal transition, you more than likely will just feel compelled to do something. To be who you are. You do not want to miss out on any more of your life. The fear tends to diminish or sometimes just go away.

This is when you know you are ready to start your external transition.
This transition involves the outer steps. Learning makeup and hair, dressing, learning how to walk and talk. Going on hormones, if you choose to do that. Hair removal. Surgeries (cosmetic and SRS, if you choose). Going full time. These steps are described in this book.

All these external transitional steps are done to make your outside match your inside.

The internal one of course continues throughout all this. The two do overlap. And of course, you can start things like dressing and making yourself up prior to beginning any kind of formal external transition. This may be all you ever want to do, and that is ok too!

Things to Ponder

Here are some questions you might want to ponder. You do not have to have answers to these all at once. These are here just as a guide to get you thinking and help you make choices that are right for YOU in your life and your transition, if you should choose to do that.

1) How long have I felt this way? Did this feeling just come up?

Do not feel in a hurry to do anything other than explore and dress if these feelings just came up. Give yourself time to find yourself. Do not be in a rush to do anything drastic or feel you need to make any decisions. Things to do in this finding yourself period would be to dress, find support groups or other TG's in your area, find a therapist, and have a little fun. You do not want to do something you cannot take back until you know what your path is. So take your time and explore.

2) What is it about being a woman that gets me excited? Is it the clothes? The sex? The peace of mind? Being myself? The attention? A deep inner and continuing desire to be a woman? This will help you choose what path is right for you in your transition and how far you want to go.

3) What do you feel like you are? A crossdresser? Transvestite? Drag queen? Shemale? Transsexual? I will briefly go over these terms again.

A crossdresser really just enjoys dressing. It makes them feel sexy or peaceful or just good about themselves. But they do not have any desire to be a woman. A Transvestite is turned on sexually by wearing woman's clothing, but, once again, has no desire to be a woman. A Drag Queen dresses more for fun or for shows. A

Shemale loves her male parts but also wants to be female. And a Transsexual truly feels like a woman inside and wants to live her life as a woman. No disrespect is meant by any of these terms. They are all fine. And you may be a combination of these. Read the "What Brought you Here" section to explore this more. Identifying who you think you are will help you know what steps you want to take.

4) How compelled do I feel to do something about this right now?

You do not have to do anything unless you want to or feel comfortable with it and feel it is right for you. You make your own timeline for this.

5) Can I wait? Or do I need to do SOMETHING now.

6) What am I willing to give up if necessary?

7) What will I gain from doing this? Peace of mind? Self respect? Happiness? Mental health? These are wonderful benefits of transitioning.

8) If you are married, do you want to stay married? Would you be willing to lose that if you had to? Not everybody loses their spouse. I have talked to many couples who have stayed married. This is not an easy question to answer. The same applies if you are seriously dating someone. Are you willing to lose that? Once again, you may not lose your partner. You never know. You may at least remain friends. There is no wrong answer. Only what is right for YOU and if you do not want to risk your marriage and want to stay as you are, that is just fine. Or

if you feel you need to do this no matter what, that is fine. It is your personal decision to make. Obviously, just do not make this decision lightly. Give it plenty of thought and do not rush into it. This is a good thing to talk over with your therapist.

9) Will you want to move? Or stay where you are? That is one way of avoiding people you know knowing about you, but not the best thing to do if you love where you live. However, if you do move, you can make a fresh start in a new area where nobody knows you. The problem with this is, you will be losing some of your support at home. There is always the phone, though, and airplanes to fly back when you want to visit.

10) Could you transition on your job? Would you be willing to change jobs or even careers? I was a consultant when I started to transition. I decided to find a permanent job with a small, open-minded seeming company. I was their only Database Administrator, so I figured I could go in there and make myself really invaluable and then when it came time to go full time, they would not want to lose me. I figured as a consultant, it might be seen as a detriment by my employer. Some clients might be uncomfortable hiring me. This may have been wrong, but I wanted to stack the chips in my favor as much as possible. So you might want to consider, are you working with clients in a sales or consulting capacity that might be uncomfortable or not as open to you? Most will be fine as long as you do the job.

Some other things to consider: Are you in kind of a rough work atmosphere? How are the people you work with? People can surprise you. People I thought would have a problem didn't and a couple I thought were my friends had a problem with it. So do not discount people. But how do you think it would be coming in to work where you are? It will be easier if you are in a professional atmosphere or work more by yourself than if you are in a more blue collar, rough work atmosphere where they might not be as accepting and give you a hard time. If you like your job and work to make yourself a likeable and valuable employee, you more than likely will be fine.

Now, these are all good questions. But they are not meant to deter you. They are things to consider so you can do some planning and find what you want to do. As I said, you do not have to answer these all.

If you truly want this, then it is worth some trouble to figure it out for yourself. You may have to make some sacrifices. You may have to make some changes. You may have to get uncomfortable (in fact you will). But it is SO worth it. Look at what you will GAIN. Peace of mind. Self love. The freedom to be yourself. Believe me, it is a terrible price to pay to not be yourself.

But take it one step at a time. You do not have to decide to end your marriage or quit your job or tell anybody or whatever. In fact, do not rush these decisions.

You do not HAVE to do anything. If you choose never to do anything other than learn to love yourself and accept who you are inside, but you are happily married and love your job and for you do not want to give anything up, that is your business and your life. It does not invalidate you. This is about what is inside you and doing what YOU choose is right for YOU. You may also just want to be part time or just dress or some other unique path that is right for you. Or you may decide that you want to live as a female. Find that path.

Remember, this is about what YOU want. You are not doing this for other people, including other people in the TG community, so do not let anybody tell you what you HAVE to do, unless it is for your safety.

Your therapist can also help you with a lot of these questions, especially with working with your spouse and children and finding what you are.

These questions will help you get an initial idea of what YOU want to do in your transition, of what is right for you and your timeline.

Transitioning is rather expensive, depending on how much you want to do. Depending on your financial situation, you may want to start saving money. Maybe do a career change. Being self employed is another option if that is something you are open to. It puts you more in charge of your destiny.

Remember, you do not have to postpone your happiness. You ARE a woman now. You can do small things. You want to put yourself in as good a financial position as possible. So do not neglect your career and other dreams. You can transition right along with that. Even if it is just practicing your voice, dressing some, developing a look. A lot of these things do not require any money.

Remember, the bulk of your transition really happens in your head. Become ok with who you are, and the rest of the transition will just naturally follow.

As I previously stated, you do not have to make a lot of decisions yet, like do you want to leave your marriage or risk it or change careers. Just start slowly. Let your subconscious work on it. Follow your gut. It will guide you to what kinds of decisions you need to make and then you can plan from there. The only thing I would recommend is getting yourself in a good financial position by saving money or choosing a good career you would enjoy. So the sooner you can start saving money (unless you are pulling in a good income already), the better. Transitioning does take money and you want to be able to do that in a healthy way.

I will make a side note here. This is no criticism of escorts. I am not passing judgment on anybody. I am not in their shoes and I understand the need to make money and how situations can become desperate so some girls turn to escorting. But escorting is not the way to go. I only bring this up as escorting is rather prevalent in the TG community as girls are trying to earn enough money to survive and also to pay for the expense of transition.

That is why I emphasize working on your career before making any drastic move. The transition will happen. It does not have to happen all at once. Once you become an escort, you have to live with that the rest of your life. It can haunt you later. Not to mention the risks. You do not know who you are meeting. The loss of self respect that accompanies being an escort - you may forget you are worth more than just your body and looks. Also, you are not young forever. Sooner or later, there will be girls younger than you and that is what a lot of the men will want. Besides, do you want to just be wanted just for your looks and your body? You have so much more to offer. Do not be lured by quick easy money. You only have one life. Respect yourself and do something that you will enjoy and demand to be loved and wanted for more than just your looks.

Happiness Now! (You don't have to postpone being happy until later)

As we transition, it is easy to get into the mindset of thinking we will be happy once we get to such and such step. Or once we do such and such a thing. Or we will be a woman once we go full time.

Do not fall into this trap. You are a woman NOW. Say that to yourself throughout the day. "I am a woman." You are happy NOW. Remember, ENJOY THE JOURNEY. Enjoy your LIFE! ALL of it! You only get one of these things, and you want to take full advantage of it and savor it!

It is kind of like what a lot of us do with the weekend. We think or say, "I can't wait for the weekend. When Friday gets here, I'll be happy." Then Friday comes. And we are so happy! Then Sunday night comes and you cannot help but feel a little let down. Two days seemed so long on Friday! Why was this weekend not life changing? I have to go back to work tomorrow. Blech. Meanwhile, during the week, we are talking with our friends, going out to eat, maybe taking a day off to go see a new exhibit at the museum, but forgetting to enjoy those things too because we keep aiming for that weekend.

This was key for me, although I did not really know what I was doing. I just LOVED transitioning. I was so excited to be moving towards my goal, to finally be taking positive steps. I just loved everything I learned and did. It felt so good to be me. I was being me. I felt free to be a woman and to let my femininity out to the fullest, even if it was only part of the time. It was such a wonderful feeling!

So enjoy this time! You ARE doing something for YOU! You are taking steps, learning to accept and love yourself more. You are learning to be YOU. You can enjoy that no matter where you are in your transition or what you are doing, even if it is strictly in your head for now. Remember, a lot of the things we DO are strictly in our head – discovering who we are, what we want to do, accepting ourselves, loving ourselves, planning, etc.

Also, throughout my transition, I literally thought of myself as female. I thought of myself as a woman all the time. I just KNEW what I was. To the outside world, I still looked like a man. To my inside world, I was a woman. And I knew I was doing something about it to make my outside match my inside. But still, I already felt like a woman. So I was not looking at any one step to make me happy or finally "turn me into a woman." Sure, I looked forward to the next step, but I was not aiming for any one step (for example, therapy, going full time, surgeries, going out the first time, etc.) to finally make me happy. I already was! I tell you, that first year of my transition was just MAGICAL. I felt so alive! I swear I looked 10 years younger. It just brought out the real me and I felt so alive and happy and at peace to be taking steps for me and finally accepting who I was and loving it. Enjoy this time! It is wonderful (as are all stages).

What a wonderful feeling to know you are a woman! Or to know you are ok for being who YOU are and to just BE who you are (whatever that is – cd, tv, ts, drag queen, gay man, etc). You can experience that NOW! You do not have to wait. You do not have to spend any money. You do not have to do anything. You already are a woman or whatever you are inside. You are very special! It is like celebrating yourself!

And if you are a TS, once you have that mindset, once you feel like a woman, think like a woman, experience being a woman on the inside, it just propels you forward in your transition.

Even if you cannot do anything, due to monetary concerns or family concerns or you need more time to prepare or you do not want to go full time or whatever, you can still experience being a woman inside. That acceptance and love of yourself is so empowering and freeing. You can let go of any self hate or self criticism, and that is a wonderful thing to do for yourself.

The way I look at it, our bodies are really just cars carrying our Spirits around. I do not mean this in a church-religious way, but we really are spiritual beings. Our bodies do not define who we are. They are something the world may see, but it is not who we really are. And our Spirits are who we really are. This may be male, female, or a combination of both. You may be an extrovert trapped in an introvert right now. Or a painter trapped in an engineer's body right now. You get the point.

The other reason you do not want to always be looking to the future for your happiness, is you will always be holding your happiness out in front of you and not experiencing it in the present. You do not want to miss out on life and enjoying your "now." You do not want to miss out on experiencing ALL of life. As I have said before, enjoy the journey! Each step is unique and fun and exciting and a joy.

Finally, if you are waiting for a certain step (such as going full time or going on hormones or having some surgery), then you are setting yourself up for a letdown. Things really do not make us happy. You have to be happy for yourself, for your own sake, with who you are. The perfect facial surgery or going full time or whatever it is for you is not going to make you happy if you are not happy with yourself. Look forward to these things of course. Enjoy them. They are joyful things to experience. However do not think you have to be "there" to be happy. What if it takes years (which some things do)? What if you cannot afford it or it is not an option for you? Do you want to be miserable then? Do not let it have that control over you. You will be setting yourself up for a letdown.

For example, if your whole life is about getting to Sex Reassignment Surgery. That is your ultimate goal. That is all that will make you happy. Once it is done. Then what? That has been your sole source of happiness and your sole goal. What do you do now? What if you are still unhappy?

Remember, have a balanced life. Have other things you are working towards and enjoying besides your transition (although you are enjoying and working towards that as well).

Learn to be happy now. Enjoy being a woman inside. Enjoy being you. Enjoy all of life! Transition, friends, family, work, hobbies, pets, all of it!

The title of this chapter sounds a little like a Seinfeld episode where George's father goes to see a psychiatrist or therapist about his stress level and the therapist tells him to say "Serenity Now!" whenever he gets stressed. So when his wife nags him, for example, he just screams "SERENITY NOW". Of course, he does not sound too serene. Always one of my favorite Seinfelds.

But that might be a nice little mantra to remind yourself when you find yourself "postponing your happiness" (as we all do at times).

Just say to yourself "Happiness Now!!!!!!!"

The School of Observation (Learning to walk, sit and act like a woman)

One of the easiest and most important ways to learn to be passable is to simply watch how women act. This is very similar to what a child does. They imitate their parents and other adults. You are in a way, like a child again, learning how to act again.

Watch how women act. How they walk. How they talk. How they hold their hands. Get into a car. Sit. Hold their faces. Of course, pick women you would like to act like when doing this!

As you begin observing how women act, you will see that women act in different ways. There are very butch ladies. Very feminine ladies. And ladies all in between. Funny ladies. Serious ladies. Ladylike ladies. Rough ladies. Etc. So you can develop your own personal style, depending on what you would like to present and act like.

If you see a lady that you admire or like the way she acts, watch what it is that you like. Then try to imitate it. It is the greatest school out there. Imitating is not hard. Human beings are natural mimics. You are a good imitator whether you know it or not.

It is a rather ironic fact that we as transgendered people often had the right habits to begin with in our early childhood. However, our parents and teachers and society trained us to hide these. We had to LEARN to act masculine many times, to act more "like a man." However, we more than likely had very feminine habits, although not always (so it is ok if you did not). Do not worry about that.

However, just as we learned to act like a man, we can learn to act like a female now. We just have to re-learn what we suppressed and hid as a child. Literally relearn what we unlearned. Or perhaps learn completely new ways of acting.

Here are a few general tips.

1) Walking

You really need to learn to walk like a lady. This can really help your passability.

Here are some things men do. They tend to walk faster and more "jerkily". They walk with their arms out and flexed a bit, like they are showing how strong they are or are ready for a fight. Some men tend to shuffle from side to side. Some men lunge as they walk.

As a woman, you need to learn to glide as you walk. Relax your shoulders. Relax your arms. Do not clench your fists ever, like men sometimes do. Walk slowly and smoothly. You can walk faster as you learn to do that and still walk gracefully, but at first, you do need to slow down your walk. However, when you are wearing heels, you really need to slow down to have a graceful and smooth walk.

Practice walking in front of a mirror. Watch how you walk. Are you walking smoothly and gracefully?

Think as you walk, "I am feminine. I am graceful. I walk smoothly. I glide as I walk." If you think this way, your body will correspond. It cannot help it. There is a mind/body connection we all have. Your body will match what you are thinking. For example, think a happy thought, and your face and body will relax and you might smile. Think of a fight you had with a coworker and what you wished you had said to him or her, and your face will probably get an unpleasant look on it and your body will tense up. Think thoughts such as "I am feminine and graceful" and your body will match as well.

It is especially important to practice walking in heels.

It is important to not start out with 6 inch heels. In fact, I would recommend avoiding heels this high period. They can really peg you as a TS and most women do not wear them. Plus, you cannot help but walk like you are in pain (usually because you are in pain – they hurt!) and awkwardly due to their height. But if you like them, that is ok. Just do not start out in them.

Start out with a nice 2 or 2-1/2 inch heel to get used to walking in heels. Walking well in heels takes practice. You will walk a little "clunky" at first. You might wobble a bit. Once again, think as you walk, "I walk smoothly and gracefully. I am feminine." Your body will start to correspond to that. Once again, do this practice in front of a mirror and watch yourself, especially from the side.

Learning to walk like a woman can take some time. You will have to unlearn some old "male" habits. But you CAN do this. Just practice, practice, practice.

2) Do not be afraid to let out your femininity or be a bit flamboyant.

In other words, feel free to talk more feminine. Talk with your hands, let your hand go limp if you feel like it. If you were what was called a "sissy" as a child (no offense is meant at ALL by that term, as I know it is used cruelly by children, but it is a term many can relate to), act more like you did then. That will give you a frame of reference for acting with more femininity. Or think of a flamboyant woman or gay man, even. Act more like that to begin with just to help you begin to let your "male acting" guard down a bit. Later you can then pull back from this and just be feminine.

Just do not overdo it and become OVERLY flamboyant (unless you just are flamboyant and enjoy that). Being OVERLY flamboyant might make you appear less passable. Sometimes at least. And as I have said before, being passable is not all it is about. This is about being happy with who you are. If you naturally have a flamboyant personality, that is just fine.

3) Getting in a car or sitting down in a chair

Make sure you keep your knees together. Get in this habit when sitting in general. Hold your skirt or dress underneath you by gently putting your hand underneath your thighs or bottom as you get in a car or sit down to hold your skirt or dress in place. When getting in the car, sit down in the seat first, with your knees together, and then gently swing your legs into the car.

4) Sitting

No more crossing your leg like a man and sitting with your ankle on the opposite knee. Make sure you keep your knees together or everybody will get a peep show, even if you are wearing pants. It just looks more lady-like to keep your knees together. Knees together and ankles crossed is a nice way to sit. You can cross you legs, but learn to do it relaxed, with one leg hanging down over the other leg as women do. Once again, watch women. See how they cross their legs. Gently lay your hands in you lap, with one hand over the other.

5) Facial expression – Remember to think, "I am a woman." Think, "I am gentle, feminine, and confident." This will show on your face. Once you get that embedded in your head (or it could just naturally be there already) and stop worrying about being pegged, your face will naturally become more feminine. Relax your facial muscles more.

Open your eyes a bit more. Make them appear bright. This will give you a more feminine appearance. THINK femininity and your face will reflect it.

Once again, your body cannot help but match in the way it will hold itself. The mind/body connection honestly does work. Do not discount it. Use it to your advantage!

Support

"The antidote for fifty enemies is one friend." ~Aristotle

This is an area that is very important. We all need some support. Oftentimes, we as transgendered people cannot count on that from our family or existing friends or coworkers, at least at first. Although there will usually be SOMEBODY at least that will support you. However, you will be surprised; more will support you than not, even if they do need time to adjust.

Support can come from friends, support groups, online chat rooms (although be careful of these as they seem to attract a lot of negative people), and your therapist. These are all great. As you transition, you do want to find a circle of friends who will support you.

And you do not need to have a HUGE circle of support, even. Even just a good friend or two will do the trick.

If you do live near a major city, look for a support group or even a Transgendered social-type group. It is good to have people to talk to that are going through what you are. However, be careful here as well. Sometimes there are people who think you should follow one path and if you do not, they will deem you not "legitimate" and they may be quite critical or exclusionary. Never let anybody tell you what to do, even another TS. Your path is your path and is what is right for YOU.

Also, if the group you hang around with starts to bring you down, then do not hang around that group. We start to think like those we hang around with.

However, there are a lot of fun and supportive TG groups out there, so seek out one of those. These groups can also be an invaluable resource for pointing you towards other resources in your area, such as doctors, therapists, TG friendly stores, etc.

If you find a TG friendly store in your area (e.g. a store that caters to crossdressers or a wig place), they might be able to point you to TG groups in your area.

There is also online for finding other transgendered people to chat with. There are TG chatrooms online (www.urnotalone.com is one place). Just be careful in these, as you may find some rather negative people taking out their frustrations online or trying to bring others down to boost their own self esteem, not to mention there is a lot of sex talk in these places (not that that is bad, but that will not give you support). However it is easy enough to ignore these people online. So just go into these chat rooms with caution. I have met some nice people online, though, and formed online friendships at least.

Also, when seeking out friends and support, try to have friends from all types of groups - straight, gay, transgendered, married, single, older, younger, etc. Do not just hang out **solely** with other transgendered people.

While we all need this support and to talk to others like ourselves, and it is good to have transgendered friends, you do not want to just have friends that are transgendered. Otherwise, you might end up thinking the whole world is against transgendered people or that life is horrible and hard. Unfortunately, this mindset does seem to predominate amongst some TG's, understandably so, but the whole world is NOT against you. Many will admire you.

Pick people you like, whether they are transgendered or not. Find open minded, positive people. Having different types of friends will help you to see there are good people in any type of group.

Also, if you are going to go full time or at least come out and tell a lot of people about yourself, it might not be a bad idea to kind of gently back away from people who you think would not be supportive. You do not have to cut them out of your life. In fact, do no do that, as they may end up being VERY supportive (people will surprise you at times). However, it is sometimes good to create a little emotional protection for yourself by backing away slightly from possibly unsupportive people prior to coming out or going full time. You want to seek out and surround yourself with open, supportive people and stay away from unsupportive people when you are at the fragile starting stage at least.

A good partner can also be invaluable. We all cannot have that right away. Your existing partner may be great. I have talked to many transgendered woman (and men) who have stayed with their existing partner. There is real love there. Many times they have been together for years and they are best friends and just want to spend their lives together, however that is.

However, your existing partner may not be able to support you as you need. They are dealing with a major change themselves. They may feel they are losing who they thought they were married to or dating. There is the sexual issue there. And they have the right to want the partner they want as well.

But when looking for a partner, if you are not lucky enough to have one, or if your current partner wants to break up or divorce (if you are at that point and want that), then look for someone with the following traits that help to support you. Some of these points have been covered in the Dating section, but I think they bear repeating here in regards to what type of partner will give you proper support.

Of course, you have to date and get to know people to see if they are like this. But love yourself enough to expect these qualities:

1) They should accept and love you JUST the way you are.
2) They should love you as both male and female, at least if you are in that stage.
3) They should love you with or without makeup.
4) They should not expect you to conform to their image of you. This is a common problem with EVERYBODY in dating. Trying to make the other person what we want them to be or them doing the same to us. It is somewhat inevitable. They have a right to want what they want, but if that something is not how you are gender wise or looks wise (because you are wonderful, remember, JUST AS YOU ARE), then they should find somebody else and so should you. Once again, it does not mean either of you are bad. You are just not the right match for each other. The ideal match really is with someone who wants someone just like you and who is just like the person you want. There are plenty of people out there looking for someone just like you.
5) They should be kind.
6) They should be there for you if they want to be serious with you.
7) They should not be paranoid that somebody will find out. You are probably a bit insecure and self conscious anyway of who you are. You want someone who will boost you up, not make you feel like you should be in hiding. These people are not bad if they are at a stage where they are worried people will know. Transgendered admirers go through their own transition. They are many times learning to accept themselves and what they like and this can take some time, understandably. However, you have been hiding your whole life. Do you want to be with someone who is ashamed of you or wants you to go into hiding again? You have come too far for that. Not that

you want to announce that you are transgendered. You just do not want to be ashamed of it or paranoid if somebody finds out.

Now, you will worry about some of these more with someone you want to get serious with (although they should always be kind and supportive of you – period). For a one time or casual dating, you may be able to overlook some of these if you choose. Only you can make that decision. But always respect yourself and expect the same in return from whomever you date, even if it is for one date. You train people on how to treat you. They will treat you the way you expect to be treated. So expect to be treated kindly and with respect.

I had various dating experiences. I did not always follow the rules above. I had to learn them. However, I learned a lot and in the process learned how I wanted to be treated. I eventually married a man who had never dated a TS before, so do not automatically rule these men out. They can be some of the best dating prospects. But they do need to follow the rules of behavior above, for the most part at least.

My husband went through the "admirer transition" I mention above. I was the first TS he ever dated. However, while he was going through that, he was also supportive of me. He was very careful of my feelings. That is the key. You want someone who realizes it is not just about their worries or fears. You are going through more than they are, and you are going through enough changes without having to worry about looking or walking or talking or whatever the wrong way so he feels self conscious. That has to be his issue and it is ok if he has it as long as he is willing to grow and support you at the same time (and you can offer him moral support as well as he goes through this transition for himself). He admitted he had guilty feelings at first and worried about people finding out. However, he was kind about that and worried more about hurting my feelings than his worries.

My point is, they do not have to be perfect (obviously nobody is). If they are kind and respectful and you have a connection you want to work on, you can really help each other get through your individual transitions to being a healthy couple.

Finally, there is one area of support I think we can all use, which you may not be thinking of, and that I would recommend for everybody: a pet. Now if you hate animals, well then this would not be for you. But if you do, and you do not have one, get a pet. If you are in an apartment, get a cat. Get a hamster if necessary, but preferably a dog or cat.

A pet will give you unconditional love throughout everything. No matter how you look, they will love you. My dog saw me as a man. Then my dog saw me as dressed up. Then she saw me go to work as a man and come home and change into a woman. Then she saw me go full Time. Then she saw me go on hormones and get breasts. She loved me the same throughout.

We often will go through many troubles with people. People can be rather fickle. They are dealing with their own issues, including handling your changes, which we understand, but it can still hurt. That cat or dog will love you through it all. There is nothing like nuzzling up to your dog or cat when you are down. And a dog especially will know when you are down and come up and lay his nose in your lap and look up at you with love. You are wonderful in his or her eyes. And you ARE (wonderful that is).

A pet also helps to take us out of ourselves. We all need something to care for and love. When you are down or feeling sorry for yourself (which we all do sometimes and that is ok!), it can be really comforting to take your dog for a walk or clean the kitty litter or just sit and pet your cat or dog.

It is Time to Appreciate and Accept our Diversity!

This section deals with releasing judgment on other transgendered people that are not like you and dealing with others in the TG community who do not accept you for who YOU are.

Realize that whatever other TG people are doing is THEIR journey. It may be different from yours. That is ok. Everyone is unique. Everyone cannot follow one exact path. Do not stress if you are not doing something someone else is doing. Whatever they are doing may not be right for you or you may not be ready to do that yet.

There is a tendency among transsexuals to call some people "not a real TS" or "oh, he's just a crossdresser", like that is something less than good. Their subtle use of "he" can be quite insulting.

Acceptance starts with ourselves. We cannot expect the world to accept transgendered people if we are not accepting each other, too busy labeling each other and criticizing each other.

I am not sure why, but there is a lot of internal prejudice in the TG community. Transsexuals look down oftentimes on crossdressers or drag queens or transvestites. Full time women look down on part time women. Post ops feel superior to pre-operative women. Etc. Not ALL, of course. I am just saying these prejudices within different groups exist in the TG community.

Prejudice and grouping people together is a natural human tendency.

I guess it is partly because as human beings, we do not like to be mislabeled. Understandably so. None of us like to be called something we are not.

Consequently, many TS's feel that crossdressers or drag queens or whatever give them a "bad name".

We all need to stop worry about what other people are doing or calling themselves. This is their choice. This is THEIR life, not yours. Let them be themselves. Do not get too caught up in labels.

You want to be who you are and be allowed to do that. Let them do the same. Just because they are different does not make them bad. And the only person that can give you personally a good or bad name is…. YOU.

The people you encounter will not care what other people are doing. They only see what YOU are doing. So you just be you and just worry about you. After all, you are the only one you have control over. Why worry over something or someone you cannot control?

These other people are living their lives and have that right. These people being different from you is not threatening you being who you are or being accepted, unless you think that is so.

We all in the TG community need to stop worrying about our differences and learn to accept and support each other. Live and let live, as the old saying goes. Somebody being who they are is not going to threaten you being who YOU are.

And do not worry about them making a "bad impression" to the world. Let people be who they are. When you start accepting people and just letting them be who they want, people will start accepting you back. It is great. Energy always mirrors back in life.

Your only job, ESPECIALLY at the beginning, is to worry about YOU. You are the only person you are responsible for. You are the only person you have control over. You are the only person whose image you need to worry about, and that image should be how YOU want to be. Figure out who you are. Be happy with it. Do not worry if you do not fit some label in the TG community. Be open to your image changing as well as you develop and grow. That is all you have to do.

If somebody else wants to call themselves a TS, and you do not feel they have "earned" that label, stop worrying about it. This is not a competition. Nobody is doing this comparison except you. You just worry about you.

And if somebody else is passing judgment on you or putting you down or trying to "invalidate" you, just realize that is their own issue. They are just showing their own insecurities and self criticism or trying to bring you down to make themselves feel better.

Treat yourself with dignity and realize you are just as good as they are and a special human being and whatever you are doing and whoever you are is OK. It is your life. You are the one who has to live it, not them. So you just do what is right for you, even if it is not the TG "norm."

Helpful Insights 2

1) **Remember that it is good to be different.**

   Everybody is different inside. However, they are usually just trying to blend in. That is a terribly price to pay. This transition will help you in all areas of your life. You will learn to be different. To be proud of who you are. To realize it is good to be the unique you. That it is painful to NOT be you. That you can do anything. This realization and new found sense of self and independence will help you to be more of you in every other area of your life

2) **Be proud of who you are, but do not feel you have to announce it.**

   You do not have to tell everybody you know. It is none of their business most of the time anyway.

   But at the same time, be ok if somebody knows. So they know you are a TS. Who cares? That is who you are, and it is wonderful! It does not make you any less of a woman.

   Like I said, you do want to blend in, and to just be accepted as woman. We all do want that. However, you also do not want to be paranoid that somebody will know. You want to be ok with that, and yet feel that you are totally female. Most people will not know as you progress further in your transition anyway.

3) **Enjoy your differences.**

   If you are always trying to be like everybody else or be perfect, you will never be happy. You are perfect just the way you are. See your differences and "imperfections" as assets, and you will be amazed at what happens to not only your own personal sense of satisfaction, but also in how people treat you. These differences and "imperfections" are part of what makes you YOU.

Do not Worry about Why TOO Much

It is human nature for us to want to categorize things and explain them. We are not comfortable "living in the mystery". So it is natural for us to wonder why we feel the way we do. To find some biological or psychological reason for being the way we are.

However, I do not believe we should spend TOO much time worrying about this. Yes we should talk with a professional therapist and handle our issues and problems. And yes, it is good to explore the "why" a bit.

However do not spend too much time or energy trying to figure out "why". The bottom line is, you feel like you feel.

There are many reasons you may be like you are – hormone imbalances in the body, XXY chromosomes, trauma in childhood, individuality, sexual desires, estrogen levels in the womb while your mother was pregnant with you, etc.

In my opinion, most of this search for reasons seems to me to be for validation. Some TS women seem to want to feel they cannot help being the way they are because of this biological reason (e.g. XXY chromosome). Many want to prove to the world why we are like we are.

Once again, you feel like you feel. That is what is most important. Not why.

There are intersexed girls or girls with XXY chromosomes. Sometimes this is presented as a more valid reason for being who they are as it is biological.

Well, what if you are not intersexed or XXY. Does this make you illegitimate? NO! Do you not feel female inside? This is what counts. How you feel inside. Whatever that is. Maybe you feel like a male who likes to express his female side or who just likes to dress. Or a gay man who finds it sexually stimulating or exciting. Or maybe you truly feel like you were a woman born in a man's body, but are not intersexed, nor have an XXY chromosome. Whatever you are is fine.

It is how you feel inside, how you identify that is what counts. Explore that (i.e. how you feel inside, how you want to live yourself) more that what the reason is. You do not need any validation. You do not need a reason to be you. You just are you.

The reason you are what you are may be biological, but you do not even need that to validate yourself. The reason may be psychological, but you do not need that to validate yourself either. Those things are nice to know or learn, but what if none of them apply to you? Does that make you a "fake TS". Are you not a woman?

Of course you are a woman, if that is how you identify inside! Being a TS is all about what you feel you are inside. Not what chromosomes you have or even what you have DONE. It is who you are inside.

Do not let anybody tell you any differently. People who try to illegitimize you because you do not have a biological reason or are different from them or not following their path are really just expressing their own insecurities and ignorance.

You are how you feel. There are as many types of transgendered types as there are transgendered people. This is about being who YOU are.

Not what you think you should be to fit in with society or the TG society.

Not what society tells you.

Not what the TS community says you should be or do.

You are OK. You are special.

You are unique.

If you are not "XXY chromosomed" or did not have a realization when you were 2 years old (which I have heard some ts's claim), or are not intersexed or whatever other girls tell you they have experienced, that does not make you any less of a woman. It is how you feel inside that counts. Your experience, is your experience. We all have a different journey to where we are today and different reasons for being here. You are just fine as you are.

Some Starting Steps for Feminizing Your Look

There are a few steps that can be taken immediately to help you appear more feminine later, without actually letting on to anybody that you are doing anything. No offense is meant by any of these tips. You do not HAVE to do these things. As I said, they are just recommendations that will start changing your body so that later you will appear more feminine when you are ready to go out as your female self.

1) If you are very overweight, start to lose some weight. This will definitely help you to look more feminine later. However, do not lose so much weight that you are bone skinny. This will make you look more boyish. Some curves are nice when you are a woman, and give you a softer look.

   For example, I am 5'10" and got down to 140 pounds at once point. Well that was nice for fitting into a smaller size, but I also lost my butt and hips and my face started to look gaunt and harder. I gained back 20 pounds, am very proportionate for my height, got my butt back (which is good if you are a woman) and also have nice curves now. My face also looks softer when I am not bone skinny. My point is, do not get bone skinny or even perfectly slender, unless that is your natural build. You just want to have a good healthy weight. Some curves are nice when you are a woman, and give you a softer look.

   Also, lose your weight in a healthy way. Do not starve yourself. Do not try to lose it too fast; lose about 1 to 2 pounds per week. Do a healthy diet. Remember, it is not worth losing your health to feminize your body. Your health should always come first. If you plan to do SRS down the road, you will want to be at a good healthy weight for that as well.

Now that you are becoming a woman on the outside, you might find yourself more susceptible to something genetic women deal with and that is poor self image or unrealistic expectations caused by looking at women on the covers of magazines (Vogue, Cosmopolitan, etc). Well, nobody looks like those women, or at least not many. I am not even sure those models look like those models! They do a lot of airbrushing and the models often are starving themselves to be that skinny, so that is not the best image to follow. My point is, do not worry if you are not that skinny or compare yourself to models on magazines or you will never be happy with your weight or body.

Once again, NO offense is meant by this tip if you are overweight. You are still a beautiful person, and if you love your weight, then you just stay right where you are and phooey with everybody else. This is just to help you appear as feminine and passable as possible later on.

2) If you are a weightlifter or very muscular, stop lifting weights. You need to lose the bulky muscle. Instead, you want to do more cardio, stretching, yoga, Pilates (great for getting a long, lithe look). You want to do exercises that give you lean muscle, not bulked up muscle. It is harder to look feminine when you have a bodybuilder physique. Now, if you like that look and you are happy with yourself, go right on ahead, of course, and keep weight lifting. I am just stating that losing bulky muscle and getting a leaner look will help to help you appear more feminine if you should go out as a woman later.

3) Start shaving your body hair. If you are married, and are not sure how to explain that, just say you like the smooth

look better. Now you can cover up a lot of body hair with clothes, and just shave your legs, so as long as you wear long sleeves and a high neck (unless you have no chest or arm hair), then just shave your legs. See the Hair Removal section for more information.

4) Start using lotion every day after you shower to start softening and firming your skin.

5) Start following the skin care tips given in the Skin Care section to start improving the look and feel of your facial skin.

These simple steps can start moving you towards a more feminine appearance without doing anything out of the ordinary.

Therapy

This step is so, so important. Therapy is such a help when you are transitioning. Do not skip this section. Even if you think you do not want to go beyond dressing, read this section (it cannot hurt to read it at least, right).

This is a section that I think is relevant to everybody. We all can use a sympathetic ear, a guiding hand, a second opinion, a personal advocate, and someone who understands gender issues and can work with us, someone who can help us discover who we are and what we want to do. Therapy can provide these and more.

This truly is one of the keys to your own personal health. Not just a step you have to take to get on hormones, get SRS, etc.

Now, I will make a confession. I went to see a therapist strictly to get on hormones and follow the Harry Benjamin standard rules when I started out. I was not necessarily opposed to therapy. I just felt that I had my head on straight and was comfortable with myself. And I was. For the most part. I just kind of figured, well I need to do this to get on hormones (at that point I was still a believer in hormones and felt I HAD to go on them – see the Hormone section for more) and get SRS, so I will go.

The bottom line was, I felt OK about who I was. I did not think I needed therapy to help me deal with my problems as I felt I was doing fine. I felt like a very well-adjusted person, and I was. But I definitely still had some issues lying underneath that I was not noticing or was ignoring Some not even related to transitioning.

My issues were mainly related to guilt. Guilt about "sinning against God." Guilt about disappointing my parents. Guilt over hurting people. Guilt over feeling selfish. Yeah I was just fine. Except for the guilt eating me up, which I was conveniently ignoring! To me, guilt was a way of life. It is kind of like when you have a chronic pain. After awhile you get used to it and do not think of it anymore.

I had a lot of guilt. For someone so confident of being ok with herself, this was rather interesting. But I think that feelings of guilt such as mine are common with transgendered people. We live our lives for everybody else. We make ourselves miserable so everybody else can be happy and comfortable. It is all very codependent.

While I am not advocating not caring about anyone but yourself, you do need to take care of yourself, or you are not doing anybody any favors. It is called self love. Are you not worthy of being happy too? Did you ask to feel this way? You will only end up resenting these people to some degree and not being the whole you. Besides which, you are not trusting them to know.

Worrying about what people will think or hurting those we love are not illegitimate concerns. They are very understandable. Relationships are important to ALL human beings. Nobody wants to hurt anyone. But when it comes at the cost of completely suppressing who you are it can be a very psychologically damaging way to live.

If you are confused about what you are or what you want to do, a therapist can help you find your way. This is VERY important. There are many transgendered people that are confused about what they are. Are they a TS or a CD or a feminine man or gay or a TV or whatever? It can be confusing. A therapist can help you sort that out.

This is very important! You do not want to do something drastic that can have long lasting, and irreversible effects like surgery or hormones without being sure this is for you. A therapist can help you figure that out. This is for your safety and protection so you do not do anything rash or something you will regret later.

Therapists can also help in many other ways.

If you are scared, they can help you deal with that.

If you do not know what to do, they can point you in the right direction and recommend resources in your local area.

They can recommend doctors and surgeons to you.

They can help you heal and love who you are.

They can help you understand (along with this book) that you are SO SPECIAL, JUST as you are.

As I said, do not worry that they are a gate keeper. They are there to help you. Not hinder you. This help, however, may include keeping you from doing something that would not be right for you. For example, going on hormones at a certain point if you are still confused as to who you are and what you want to do. This step is there for your safety. And they are on your side.

When picking a therapist, you have to find one that you feel is a good match for you. Therapists have different personalities and styles. You may have to go to a few therapists to find one that you feel comfortable with.

Are you more comfortable with a man or woman? Do you like someone to tell you what to do and guide you more or to listen more and let you talk things out? Do you like blunt-talking people or more soft-spoken people? We all have different tastes and styles. But what it really gets down to is, how do you feel in the session with this person. Give it a few sessions. If at the end of a few sessions, you do not feel comfortable with this person or do not like their style, find another therapist. You need to feel comfortable with this person and trust them.

To find a therapist, you want to find one who specializes in "gender issues". They may call themselves a "Gender Therapist". This does not need to be the only thing they deal with, but at least one of them.

To find a therapist, you can check with any local TG support or social groups in your area. If there are none of these, check with a local gay and lesbian (GLBT) group. Sometimes therapists that serve these groups also work with transgendered people. You can also check online. Just do a search for "gender therapist" and your area.

Remember, this step is there for your help. Therapy is not the answer to all problems, but it can be a real help in the right situations, such as with gender issues.

You will come out of therapy a healthier, more positive person with a real sense of yourself.

Helpful Insights 3

1) **When making decisions on clothes, makeup, hair, style, walking, talking, less is more.**

Remember, go a bit extreme to get the hang of something, then pull back a little. Slutty may be fun and attract men, but it also makes you look unpassable usually. If you want to look that way, that is OK. Seriously. BE yourself. Who cares what people think. But this book is about helping you to blend and be passable. Genetic woman who dress slutty attract attention, and not necessarily good attention. So it is not just you. (Of course, there are always occasions to look a little slutty for your special someone, but we are talking day to day.)

2) **Do not worry about what you cannot change. Instead, see it as an asset.**

This applies to ANYTHING you cannot change – your height, for example, or the size of your hands or feet. These things are what they are, and you cannot change them. So, see them as an asset and appreciate them.

If you cannot change something, why make yourself miserable hating it or worrying about it? Concentrate on what you can change or what you have already that you appreciate.

I know I used to be self conscious about my height (I am 5'10" and even taller in heels, obviously). I seemed to be taller than practically everybody at work and most people I met. So I would start to stoop to make myself appear shorter, or not wear some shoes I liked because the heel was too high.

Then I started realizing that I could not change my height. So I started to look for the good in it. I thought, "Supermodels are tall and wear heels. They are not self conscious about it. Why should I be? My height helps me maintain a slimmer figure easier. Being tall can be a distinct advantage."

I also found that a lot of people actually liked my height. Some even wished they could be as tall as me.

Once I started looking for something positive in something I had once viewed as a negative, I found those positives and stopped being self conscious. I even developed a lot of confidence in my height. I now really appreciate being so tall!

Search for the positives in a similar manner to this whenever there is something about your body that you dislike, but cannot change.

Dressing

I think dressing is one of the first areas everybody wants to get into, if they have not already. And it is a lot of fun!

Clothing is one of those immediate ways you can express your female side, and is probably something you have done or wanted to do for a long time.

But you need to determine a couple of things here first so you will know what type of clothes to buy:

1) Do you care if you are passable or not
2) Do you just want to dress up sexy and have fun

Depending on how you answered the above two questions, your dressing style could be quite different.

Dressing is a place where you can develop your own personal style. There is no one way to dress. Look at genetic women. They dress in all styles. However, what you want to do is find a clothing style that expresses who you are, and fits the situation you are in.

Sexy, slutty, or outrageous clothes can be fun, but really, those are not appropriate anywhere but a club. They will make you stand out and give people the wrong impression to boot.

Slutty is not passable in general. I mean no insult by that at all to those who enjoy slutty clothes. It just does make it harder to blend and is what society stereotypes the TG community as wearing. So wear those types of clothes to the clubs if you really want to wear that would be my recommendation. By all means have fun, just do it in the appropriate setting.

This does not mean that you cannot be sexy, and yet tasteful. A nice pair of heels and hose and a tasteful skirt can be very sexy, believe me, and still tasteful.

So, what is your style? Conservative? Feminine? Tomboyish? Classy? Dresses and Skirts? Suits? Jeans? Are you more of a slacks and top girl or a dress or skirt girl. All these are good.

The natural inclination is to go out and buy a bunch of ultra sexy clothes. There is nothing wrong with this. Get it out of your system if you need to. If you enjoy it, then do it. You have been denying yourself your whole life. Have fun.

Just realize that down the road, there is a place for those things, and you will want to wear them less and less, just like genetic women do. For example, you will not want to wear those to work or when your family first sees you later on.

When starting out, you might want to cover up more skin. Especially if you cannot shave your body due to marriage or something similar. Although you will probably have to shave your legs at least. Buy dresses or outfits with a high neck and long sleeves perhaps. Wear slacks or tights if you cannot shave your legs. There are even opaque hose you can wear (which are kind of like flesh-colored tights) if you cannot shave your legs.

There are plenty of online clothing stores that cater to the TG community. Do a Google or Yahoo search of "Crossdressing Store" or "Drag Queen Store" or whatever key words you can think of and you will bring up a bunch of web sites. Browse through those. Have fun. They have clothes, shoes, lingerie, pantyhose, etc for you.

When picking shoes, do not go for a real high heel unless you are shorter. If you are 5'10" or above, stick with a 2-1/2" heel. 3" at the most. If you go higher, you will be too tall. However, do not be self conscious about your height. Remember, you cannot change your height, so embrace it. Supermodels are tall and wear heels, so can you. Just do not go too high.

It also tends to start making you look a bit more "slutty" and less passable if you have super high heels on. If you are shorter, you can go with a higher heel. Even then, you do not want to look too slutty. As with my previous clothing comments, if you want to have fun and wear a super high heel and look real sexy, that is fine. Have fun. Just try to confine it to the clubs or home if passability is a goal of yours.

As far as picking out your shoe size, women's sizes are a little bigger than men's. So a starting rule of thumb is to add one full shoe size to your men's size to find your women's shoe size. For example, if you currently wear a size 10 man's shoes, you would probably wear a size 11 woman's shoe.

There are shoe stores online and in many big cities that also cater to the TG community. They will carry women's shoes in bigger sizes. That can be a problem sometimes as many shoe stores only carry women's shoes up to size 10 or 11 maybe. The TG clothing stores online also carry larger shoe sizes.

As far as clothing sizes, look at the chart below. If you are shopping at a CD or TG clothing store online, they will usually have sizing charts to help you as well. But for general reference, see the table on the next page to help determine your woman's clothing size.

	Misses 5'4" to 5'7"		Petite 4'11" to 5'3"		Tall: 5'8" to 5'11"	
Order Size	2	4	6	8	10	12
Easy Fit Size	XS		S		M	
Bust	32 - 32 1/2	33 - 33 1/2	34 - 34 1/2	35 - 35 1/2	36 - 36 1/2	37 - 38
Waist	23 1/2 - 24	24 1/2 - 25	25 1/2 - 26	26 1/2 - 27	27 1/2 - 28	28 1/2 - 29 1/2
High hip	31 - 31 1/2	32 - 32 1/2	33 - 33 1/2	34 - 34 1/2	35 - 35 1/2	36 - 37
Low hip	34 - 34 1/2	35 - 35 1/2	36 - 36 1/2	37 - 37 1/2	38 - 38 1/2	39 - 40

Order Size	14	16	18	20	22	24
Easy Fit Size	L		XL		XXL	
Bust	38 1/2 - 39 1/2	40 - 41	41 1/2 - 43	43 1/2 - 45	45 1/2 - 47	47 1/2 - 49
Waist	30 - 31	31 1/2 - 32 1/2	33 - 34 1/2	35 - 36 1/2	37 - 38 1/2	39 - 40 1/2
High hip	37 1/2 - 38 1/2	39 - 40	40 1/2 - 42	42 1/2 - 44	44 1/2 - 46	46 1/2 - 48
Low hip	40 1/2 - 41 1/2	42 - 43	43 1/2 - 45	45 1/2 - 47	47 1/2 - 49	49 1/2 - 51

Women's Clothing Size Chart

Now, eventually, you are probably going to want to shop at a regular department store for clothes. This might seem a bit scary at first. Especially if you are part time, which of course, you more than likely will be when you first start shopping.

Let me tell you a few things to help you feel more comfortable shopping in public.

First off, remember, people are too busy doing their own shopping. They are not paying too much attention to you.

Second, men buy clothes for their wives and girlfriends all the time. Nobody is going to think a thing of you walking into the women's section if you are still dressed as a man. They will just think you are shopping for somebody else.

So just march in there like you are supposed to be there. Shut out everybody else. Just walk around and look. And if you feel self conscious when talking to a sales clerk, tell him or her, "Oh, I think my wife or my girlfriend will like this" if it makes you feel more comfortable. I got really good at that. And I never dated women, by the way, but I said it with a straight face. So see, anybody can do that! Then, after awhile, I stopped even doing that. I just shopped and stopped wondering what people were thinking and nobody ever EVER gave me a hard time or a second glance even.

The next problem when shopping in public (if you are part time) is how do you try on the clothing to see if it fits? This can be tricky too, but not impossible. Here is what I used to do. I would find a skirt or dress I liked. I would pretend like I was buying it for somebody as a gift. (By the way, this is a mind game I played with myself strictly in my head – I am not telling anybody this, but thinking this way helped me remain calm and look confident). Then I would walk over to the men's section holding the dress or skirt over my arm like I was buying that for somebody and I would look at pants or something. Then I would take the pants into the men's dressing room with them draped over the dress and pretend like I was going to try on the pants. Then, once in the dressing room I would try on the dress. Easy. Sure it is a little nerve wracking at first. But you will get used to it. After awhile, there is nothing to it.

Another trick to do is just mind your own business. Concentrate on your shopping. Do not make eye contact with anybody. Pretty much just ignore everybody but the sales clerk when you buy whatever you are buying, and they will all ignore you too. Once again, everybody is too busy doing their own shopping and worrying about their own problems to notice or worry too much about you.

Once you go full time, this is not an issue. You can just march into a store and shop and try on clothes like any other lady. Just make sure you march in like you think you belong there and do not be the least self conscious and you will be fine.

If you plan on going full time, you will want to start building up your wardrobe over time. It can be expensive. You are basically maintaining two wardrobes for awhile – a men's and a women's (and possibly some androgynous clothes as well). I used to go out on my lunch hour and hit the sales while I was still working undercover as a man. It was fun. It is one of those things you can do that gives you happiness even if you are not totally living as you like (for example, having to live part time when you want to live full time). Over time, I built up quite a good wardrobe so when I went full time, I was set.

Clothing is fun. It is something you can do FOR YOURSELF. A way to treat yourself. A step you can take towards your dreams each time you buy a new dress or scarf or pair of shoes or whatever.

You may also be wondering how you hide your "bulge".

Most clothes will be loose enough there where nobody will see a thing. Also, just remember, if somebody is staring at your crotch, who has the issue? NOT YOU! So do not worry about it.

However, what can we do to hide things there?

The first thing you can do is to avoid buying a lot of clothes that are "clingy" in that area. Spandex or sweats are not a good idea either as they will not hide anything. There are certain materials you will find that cling to every curve of your body. Avoid those. You can still buy form fitting dresses.

The second thing you can do is to simply wear control top pantyhose (or even regular pantyhose will work often). The pantyhose will "hold you in". Easy, simple step to take.

The third thing you can do is to "tuck". You can also wear what they call a "gaff" (any stores you find online catering to crossdressers, transsexuals and drag queens will carry these) to give yourself a smooth appearance, but you will still need to tuck.

With tucking, you will need to push your testicles up into your body (there is a little opening there you can feel) and then tuck your penis underneath. You can tape it there if you like or use a gaff.

If this makes you squeamish, do not worry. You may not have to tuck. I never bother tucking. Pantyhose do all the holding in I need and if I am wearing pants, it is hardly visible. Once again, I figure, if you are looking at my crotch, that is your problem. Nobody has ever seemed to notice though. Keeping your knees together when you sit will also help hide things there if you are a bit self conscious.

Most of the time you will not need to tuck. Just experiment and see.

A couple of last notes and cautions:

Rememember ONE thing. Clothes, like every other "thing", do not MAKE you a woman. You already are a woman. So you do not have to be in women's clothes to be a woman.

Also remember, if you just enjoy wearing women's clothing, you do not necessarily have to transition. I think some girls get confused. They enjoy dressing up and having fun and may even like to dress up as a woman sexually. But look inside. Do you really want to BE a woman, with all that entails?

Have you always had the desire to be a woman? Or have always or sometimes had the desire to dress up? Those are two different things. Yes, clothing is part of being a woman and a fun part. But there has to be more than just that for you to go through something as serious as a transition. So just remember that. Have fun dressing if that is all you like. That is ok! If you want to be a woman, do that too!

Makeup

"I've never seen a smiling face that was not beautiful." ~Author Unknown

Makeup is a fun area. This is a place where you can express yourself and enhance your beauty. Give yourself a unique look. This is also an extremely feminizing process obviously. You can mask some "masculine" features you perhaps do not like as well.

Now, as with clothes and hair, remember, the slutty, bold look will hurt your passability. Less is more in this area, as far as passability goes. But if you want to do that, it is ok. And of course, you can wear more subdued makeup most of the time and save the bolder "sexier" makeup for things like dates or special nights with your significant other. Be yourself. Just remember, what men think looks "hot", is not necessarily what will make you look like a natural woman or passable.

However, have a little fun if you want to experience that. You have denied yourself your whole life, so go for it. Just do not make the slutty look your long term look.

However, this book is partly about how to be a passable woman, so I am going to give you some tips here on how to use makeup to enhance your look and be more passable using makeup.

To enhance your look, as I have stated before, you want to remove the hair on your face or get started on that as soon as possible. However, if you do not want to do that (for example if you just want to dress or stay part time) or cannot afford that yet or you are just starting, that is ok. You can cover with makeup. You just have to wear a full coverage foundation. You will also need to shave closely prior to putting your makeup on. If you have a heavy beard, you are going to have to shave a couple times a day unfortunately. A beard (if it is dark) seems to really pass through makeup, the shadow at least. If you have a light beard, you should be ok with once a day. I know it is a pain to shave twice a day, but this is very important to your passability.

The first thing to realize is, you need to experiment and practice with makeup. Find what looks best on you. How to put on eyeliner. How to apply blush. How to put on mascara. Somebody can tell you, but it takes practice, and that is part of the fun. Nobody else will be putting your makeup on you day to day, so it is kind of like learning to ride a bike. You just have to get on there and keep trying until you get it right and develop the look you like on yourself.

Now, remember, I had nobody to tell me how to put makeup on. So I was really just learning as I went and having to teach myself how to put on makeup.

So the first time I put on makeup, I bought some mascara (black), slapped that on my eyelashes, getting it all over the skin around my eyes, and then used the same mascara to do my eyebrows. I had a brown wig on. How do you think that looked? Sex-ay right? Not at all!

Of course, I was kind of thrilled just to see mascara on my self. Talk about instant feminizing. Not to mention lipstick. Plus, I was all by my little self in my bathroom, so I could make mistakes and play and look "bad" or outrageous and nobody would see it but myself and my dog. So do not worry if you put your makeup on at first and do not like the way you look or that you do not look passable or that you are putting it on wrong. Just have fun! The only way you will learn how to put on your makeup and what looks good on you is by practicing and having fun.

After my initial makeup trials, I did learn how to put on makeup and now have a very natural, tasteful look with my makeup. I have learned a lot of great tricks with putting makeup on, so you can read on without fear of looking like a clown.

First off, you will need to get the makeup.

The first thing you will need is a good foundation, unless you have no beard. You need something that gives complete coverage ("full coverage makeup"). Max Factor has a foundation called Pan-Cake that is very good for this. However, there are other complete coverage foundations. Just find one that you like and fits in your price range. Do not buy something super expensive the first time, unless money is no object. You are trying to find your color match at first and learning to play with makeup and learn to play it out, so if you would like a more expensive foundation from the Department store, those are great, but my recommendation would be experiment with putting the cheaper makeup on first, then go into the store and buy a foundation there.

You can find foundations in the drug stores, Walmart, etc from many cosmetic companies (CoverGirl, Revlon, etc), or you can go to a Department Store for higher end makeups.

There are great foundations now you can even order over the phone. Bare Minerals is a good foundation you can order via the phone, for example, although I have not used it myself, but have heard good things from some women I know.

You can also order through local makeup distributors such as Avon, Merle Norman (who are very TS friendly I have heard) and Mary Kaye.

Foundations can be applied simply with your fingers, but for many (like Pan-cake) and for best results, you will want to use a small makeup sponge to apply it. You can find these right in the makeup section of your local drugstore or Walmart (or at the

Department store if you are buying your makeup there). They are right there in the makeup section.

When picking a color, pick one that is as close as possible to your own skin tone. If possible, hold the color up to your face and look in a mirror. Now this takes some experimentation too. The color on the container will not exactly match how it goes on your face, but it will give you a good idea. In the department stores, they can help you pick a color by putting it right on your face and you will get a really good match.

To apply the foundation, just wet the sponge a little and rub a little of the foundation on the sponge. Work from your nose on out. Use short soft little strokes. Do not just rub it all over your face in one big stroke.

Follow the same procedure if using your fingers to apply instead of a sponge. However, with your fingers, take a small amount and dab it on a few places on your skin (e.g., forehead, nose, cheeks, chin) and then just lightly spread it around.

With either method of applying the foundation you are not trying to rub it INTO your skin. You are just distributing the makeup over your face. You can apply more foundation in areas that need more coverage.

To soften your look a bit after putting foundation on and help hold the makeup in place, a powder is great. This is an optional step. The foundation alone may be just fine for you.

Once again, find a powder that is as close to your own skin tone as possible. Get a nice powder brush if it is a loose powder, or some have the little powder applicator inside. You can also use pressed powder in a compact. These are nice for when you go out to pat on a bit to take shine off your face or just freshen your look.

When you put the powder on with a powder pad, do not rub it all over you face. It will make it look cakey and kind of fake. Instead, pat it on. Pat, pat, pat, pat, pat all over your face. It will give you a nice soft look.

Unfortunately, we all have different skins (oily, dry, sensitive, blemishes, different skin tones), so it will take a little experimentation on your part to find what foundation works for you as different foundations work better on these different types of skin. Foundation is tricky, but once you get it right, it is key to helping you look your best.

Now, at this point in my life, I do not wear foundation anymore. I have had the hair on my face removed (mostly, except for some blonde remaining hairs) and I take really good care of my skin (see the Skin Care section for advice), so I can get away with this now. But I could not always. But if you can get to this stage, it is great. Foundation is a pain in general and can feel heavy on your skin. But if you cannot, that is ok too. Foundation is there to help.

The next step is to take a look at your face. What are its strengths? What do you like? Do you have nice full lips, a pretty smile? You will want to accentuate your lips. What about your cheekbones? Your eyes? If you do not like anything, then go for your eyes. Makeup will make any eyes striking and pretty.

And if you cannot find anything you like about your face, I want you to go to the mirror right now and tell yourself how beautiful you are and what a beautiful woman you are, because you are. This is a great thing to do in general anyway to boost your self image – talk positively to yourself in the mirror. All kinds of successful people and celebrities do this "mirror exercise" and talk positively to themselves in the mirror. Try it!

Now I always think it is good to bring out your eyes. This is where the bulk of your makeup will go. You will want to get the following items:

1) A good eye liner. I prefer a pencil. You can sharpen it and get a good thin line then and it is easier to apply. However, you may find you like the "marker' or liquid liners. Liquid liners can be difficult to apply, but they can give you a dramatic line. But for simplicity of application and best results, I do not think you can beat a simple eyeliner pencil. I would choose black or black/brown for now. You can experiment a bit with colors later, but for now stick with these two colors. They always work no matter what your coloring or what you are wearing. If you have blonde, black, grey or white hair, I would go with the black. If you are a brunette or redhead, go with the brown/black. But do what makes you feel best – even if it is a color eyeliner. Makeup is about helping you feel pretty and confident.

2) A good mascara. Get a volumizing one if you have thin lashes. All the major cosmetic manufactures have one. I do not recommend false eyelashes – at least for day to day wear. They really can make you look fake.

3) A good eyebrow pencil. Try to get a color that matches your natural hair color as close as possible. If you are blonde, go with a soft brown (not a dark brown), or you will lose some dramatic effect. If you have white or grey, I would go with a soft black or grey color.

4) Blush. This is an important step that I neglected for a long time because I thought it looked fake. I associated it with the old rouge women used to use. But there are all kinds of soft powder blushes now. Blush really gives you a glow and makes you look younger. A little bit goes a long way. You want to swirl some on a brush (you can get a brush in the makeup department of any drugstore or department store) and then smile and apply it to the apples

of your cheeks and then go down a little to accentuate your cheekbones or give you the appearance of cheek bones. Choose a color that is complimentary to your colors. Pink or burgundy if you have a "cool" complexion, something with a little more orange or rusty color in it if you are "warm". Choose a darker color if you want to be more dramatic. Softer if you want to be more natural. If you have a wide nose you want to camouflage a bit, just lightly brush a LITTLE light-colored blush on the sides of your nose and it will make it appear thinner. Cool trick I learned early on.

5) Lipstick. This is another area to play. If you have thin lips, use a lighter color. This will make your lips look fuller. Darker colors make your lips look thinner in general. Like blush, use a darker color for a more dramatic look and a lighter color for a more natural look. You will go through some shades of lipstick finding one you like. You will probably want to have at least a couple of different shades of lipstick to go with different outfits and different looks (lighter shade for daytime and more natural, darker shade for going out).

I would stay away from too bright a red. Only a few women can really carry that off. I tend to either feel like I look like a clown or like a street walker, neither of which is the aim I am going for. And yet, I have seen women it looks just great on. I think there are two keys with red. You have to be confident enough to wear it and you have to have the right coloring. I tend to think it looks best on women with naturally black hair and white skin. Everyone else tends to need some variation of the red to make it blend with their coloring.

6) Eye shadow. You do not have to wear eye shadow. If you want to add some color above your eyes, then it is great. If you have deep set eyes, I would not use eye

shadow as it will make your eyes appear even deeper set. If you do still want to use eye shadow, then use a neutral colored (e.g. champagne or flesh colored) and that will make your eyes "pop" more. If you have big eyelids that are not deep set, then feel free to experiment with different colors. Browns, roses, neutrals and lighter colors look most natural, but experiment and have fun.

You may also want to start doing your nails. This can help to feminize your hands. Even just having them nicely manicured will help your hands appear nicer. You can also use "fake nails" (e.g. press on) that you can buy at any drug store for a night out as your female self. Even if you do not have time or do not want to do your nails on a regular basis, you can always put on a little colored nail polish for the night, and that small step alone will feminize your hands a bit.

Do not forget to use a good lotion on your hands every day to help them appear younger and to feel softer.

And that is it. The bottom line is experiment. We all are unique in our tastes and natural colorings. Play with different types of makeup to find what works best for you and makes you feel good, as makeup should.

Remember less is more when going for passability.

You want to compliment your beauty. Not overwhelm it with a lot of heavy makeup.

Lighter colors are better than darker colors for daytime.

Keep experimenting and playing and having fun and you will develop your own unique, beautiful style.

Skin Care

Proper skin care is an often neglected part of passability I think. It can make you look younger, soften your skin, even diminish the need for makeup. As a woman, you need to start taking good care of your skin (if you are not already). Proper skin care will make your skin softer, help you appear younger and more feminine.

Proper skin care really does not have to be a big pain. It can become a simple part of your routine. The main thing you want to do is wash your face (not with soap) twice a day (morning and night), and moisturize it afterwards. You need to wash your face in the morning to wash the impurities that your skin expels overnight while you are sleeping. You need to wash and cleanse your face at night to remove dirt and makeup. Do not sleep with your makeup on. This is bad for your skin.

For your body, apply a good lotion all over your body every day after showering. This will keep your skin soft and firm. I would also recommend using a nice moisturizing body wash to clean instead of soap to help further moisturize and soften your skin.

These simple, basic steps for your face and body will really help to soften your skin and give it a younger, more feminine look. I will talk a bit more in detail about a specific regime you can use in a bit, but those are the general steps.

The other thing you want to do is to AVOID TANNING. If you are already tanning, stop. Tanning is one of the worst things you can do for your skin. It will age your skin tremendously over time. Not to mention the risk of skin cancer. If you want to tan, there are plenty of great self tanning towels and sprays out there. Use those. But do not sit in the sun or at a tanning booth.

Also, eat more salads and fresh fruits and vegetables. These are "skin food". Our skin reflects our inner health, and eating a lot of fruits and vegetables will not only improve your health, but also help you have healthier, more radiant skin over time.

Now, on to some more details on skin care. I have always had to take care of my skin since I was fortunate enough to start getting pimples at the ripe old age of 11. And I did not really stop getting pimples until I was 30. So, I learned to take good care of my skin.

I have tried many types of skin care over the years, some expensive, some not, and here is what I have found to be the most effective and quite reasonable to boot! My skin looks better than it did on any other regimen with what I am about to list, and I think you will be pleased with the results if you follow this. If you do not like this regimen, just remember the basics, wash your face morning and night and put on a good moisturizer each time, using whatever you find works best for you. Play with different products until you find what works best for you.

However, here is what I use:

Cleanser: 1 Box Oil of Olay Daily Facial Cleansing Clothes (for evening) and 1 Oil Olay Renewal Cleanser (you can get both at Walmart for less than $5 for a one month supply) for the morning.

Moisturizer: Oil of Olay Total Effects with Sunscreen (I use day and night, but use for the daytime at a minimum)
Night of Olay Cream (Around $6 for a 1-1/2 to 2 month supply) – Get the Pink, not the White Cream. This stuff is amazing for moisturizing and firming your skin overnight and very reasonable.

Shaving cream that conditions and softens your Skin – You can still use a men's shaving cream. This does not make you masculine or a man. These creams just tend to soften a beard more effectively than women's shaving creams do I found. Once most of your hair is removed, you can pretty much just do a quick run over your skin with a razor with whatever you are cleansing your face with. This is where I am now, as I only have a few hairs left on my face.

Here is what you should do:

Morning:

Cleanse your face with the Daily Renewal Cleanser or whatever cleanser you are using. Two pumps is enough. Wet your face first with warm water, then shave. Then re-wet your face with warm water and pump the cleanser onto your fingers and rub all over your face. Do not scrub, just rub gently to remove all the oils and dirt. Then rinse thoroughly. Splash the water, rather than rubbing the water over your face, to rinse. Rinse until all the cleanser is removed. Your skin should almost be "squeaky".

Put a small dab of the Olay Total Effects (or whatever moisturizer you choose) on your finger. A small dab goes a long way. You will see after you use it. Then dot it on your forehead, nose, cheeks, between your lips and nose and your chin. Then gently spread the moisturizer around your face. Do not rub hard. You just want to distribute it over your face so your skin can absorb it. Rub in light circular motions with the tips of your fingers.

Put a little chapstick on your lips to moisturize them or if you are going to wear lipstick, you can skip the chapstick, as the lipstick will moisturize your lips.

Nightime

Cleanse your face with the Oil of Olay Daily Cleansing Cloths. Just put a little water on it, rub it together to lather it up a bit, then just run it all over your face. These are great for removing makeup too, including mascara. Just run them over your eyelids to remove mascara and eyeliner. Rinse the cloth again to wash out the soap and wet it more, then rinse your face off with the cloth. Your skin will be so refreshed and just glow. These things are incredible! I really would use these at least once a day.

Put some of the Olay Total Effects (or other moisturizer) on (you can skip this if you want, but I recommend it if you can). Then take a SMALL amount of the Night of Olay (the pink stuff) on your finger and dab that all over your face and then spread it around.

It is very important to put a good moisturizer like the Night of Olay on as your skin repairs overnight. So you want to use something that moisturizes and firms as you sleep. You will get the best results at night.

Put on some chapstick to moisturize your lips and protect them overnight.

And that is it!

Keeping your skin moisturized will really help it to stay or become supple and you will have firmer, younger looking skin. As you pick moisturizers and cleansers, remember it is always better to have skin that is a little oilier (but not oily) then dried out. Dried out skin will age your skin and you will get more wrinkles. You can always blot some shine away with a little powder if it bothers you, but it will usually just give you a lovely glow. Of course, perfectly balanced (neither oily nor dry) skin is best, but it is sometimes hard to achieve this perfectly.

Do not forget the skin on your body. Once again, use a good lotion for your body. You want to moisturize your WHOLE body every time after you shower or bathe. Hormones do soften your skin, but so will a good lotion used daily. Just find a lotion in your budget and to your liking. Pick one with a pretty scent if you do not mind smelling a little girly. It is a nice way to pamper yourself and feel feminine and soften your skin at the same time. Moisturizing regularly will also firm up your skin.

Hair

"The hair is the richest ornament of women." ~Martin Luther

Hair is a simple and yet complicated area. It is one of those things that can make us look instantly more feminine. By growing it out, or by our styling, or even by color. Or by getting a wig or hairpiece.

If you have thick hair that grows fine, first off I would like to say that I hate you. Ok, I should not have typed that. OK, I really do NOT hate you, but I envy you. I admit it! I started losing my hair at 18 unfortunately. It was very traumatic, as I am sure anyone who has lost their hair can sympathize with. Thus my continuing jealousy of full-head-of-hair people. (Note to self: Make appointment with therapist about continuing hair issues.)

But seriously, if you have a full head of hair, that is GREAT. You can just grow your hair out whenever you are ready to start appearing more female in front of people. It is a great way of very subtly starting to feminize yourself in front of people if you plan on coming out later.

However, I realize those of you with hair do not need a lot of advice here. You just need to grow your hair out however you want and have fun with it. You might just have to wear a wig as it grows out is all. But if it grows pretty fast, just let it start growing. Men wear their hair longer sometimes. It is not that big a deal, unless you work somewhere that has a strict code on hair length, in which case you might need to wear a wig when not there until you switch to full time.

The rest of this section will be devoted to those who are part time, cannot grow their hair, have lost your hair, or do not want to grow your hair out (even if you have a full head of hair) and need another option.

The first option is, of course, wigs. There are plenty of wig places out there, and this is where you will want to start. Have some fun with this, and get a style you have always wanted.

Do a search online for "wigs". You will find lots of wig stores. Or if you feel comfortable with it, go to a local wig place. In bigger cities there are even places that cater to the TG community. It is great to go in some place in person as you can try on different wigs to see what looks best on you.

Do not worry too much about passability at first, if you want to have some fun and try some wild or fun styles. I am a firm believer in having some fun and getting things out of our system that we always wanted to experience. So if you want a long wig down to your waist, go for it. However, they will not be the most passable style in the long term.

Eventually you will want to go with a wig style that is short (not short short, we are talking a woman's short) to medium length (shoulder length or a bit below the shoulder) for best passability.

When picking a wig color, stay away from the extreme colors – jet black and platinum blonde, unless these are your natural hair colors. Otherwise, the color will definitely make you look unnatural. If you want to get one for fun, go for it. Just do not make that your main wig. Browns usually look the most natural.

You will want to pick a color that is suited to your natural coloring. A color closest to your natural hair color will look most natural as this will naturally match your skin tone and coloring. It does not have to match your exact hair color, but be a little close to it. However, other colors can match as well. Feel free to try something new and see how it looks. Just realize the bolder or further from your natural color, the more chance it will clash with your natural coloring and you might not look as passable.

So go with browns if you are a brunette. Strawberry or medium blondes if you are a blonde. Red if you are a natural redhead. If you have jet black hair naturally (and the related skin tones), go for black then. That is fine, of course.

When picking a style, go natural. There are plenty of hair style books out there. If there is a wig place near you, go and try some on. Most of these wig places are pretty open. They have a lot of cd and tg clients, trust me.

But if you are not comfortable with that or feel you live in a not so open area, get a digital photo of your face and go to www.thehairstyler.com. This is a very cool website as you can try hundreds of hairstyles out on your face. See how they look on you. It is fun, and you can get an idea of the type of hairstyle that would look good on you. All for a very low nominal fee – very affordable.

Once again, resist the urge to look slutty or too sexy or extreme. This may attract men or be fun, but it will also attract the wrong kind of attention as well if your goal here is to look natural. If you want to get an outrageous or slutty looking wig for the club or parties or for home, go for it. Nothing wrong with that. But we are talking about day to day use. And there are plenty of natural hairstyles that are sexy too.

You want a hairstyle that compliments you. That enhances your beauty. Good color. Good style. Comfortable.

Wigs are great for your part time period or if you just do not ever want to go full time or anything. Or if you have lost your hair or your hair will not grow out. They can give you a great instant hairstyle. And wigs have SO improved over the years. There are so many natural ones. Even genetic women wear them more and more. They are fun! So enjoy. This is a fun area. There is no "shame" in wearing a wig anymore. And if anybody looks down on you for wearing a wig, thumb your nose at them and be proud of who you are! That is THEIR problem, not yours.

Now, there are many of us that lost our hair and have to find an alternate solution. I was one of those, starting when I was a senior in high school, believe it or not. What was so sad was I had the thickest, waviest, nicest hair up until then, and I HATED it because it was so thick and wavey (kids called me brillo hair!).

Well I sure would take that thick wavy hair back, but unfortunately, it waved goodbye.

If you have lost your hair or are losing it now, you know how devastating this is. We all have a certain amount of self esteem tied to our hair, as society places so much emphasis on a good head of hair. And for some reason, it is socially acceptable to make fun of someone for losing their hair.

It is even more devastating when you want to be a woman. You may wonder how are you going to do this now if you are losing your hair? It almost seems like the Universe taunting you and giving you more proof you are not a good woman at that point.

Well I have gone through all kinds of solutions to this problem over the years, and now you can benefit from my mistakes and what I have learned.

I have worn wigs. I have had bad hairpieces. Better hairpieces. Really natural hairpieces.

I have tried topicals. Unless you just have a small amount of balding though and slight receding, these do not work too well. But if you just have some thinning, go for it. The earlier you start with topicals the better. These work best when you have a little thinning on top. Not as well if you have a receding hairline, although they are always making improvements, so this may not be true by the time you read this. Rogaine is one of the best known of these. You can buy it in most drug stores anymore. Propecia is another topical. However, do a search online to find other options if that does not work well for you.

You can also get transplants. These can be very expensive, so if your budget is limited or if you have lost a lot of hair or do not have really thick hair in the back or sides (which is where they will take the hair from), then this may not be a good option for you.

However, if you have lost a lot of hair, and do not necessarily want to wear a wig or do not want to mess with topicals or hair transplants, but still want a somewhat permanent solution, there is good news: You can get a great quality custom made hair system now for under $250. Considering I have spent thousands, TENS of thousands in fact, over the years on hair replacement systems, this is good news.

Do not spend this much money. You do not have to. For years, the hair replacement places had me convinced that I had to go there to get these things put on and maintained. That they had to do it. That these things were very expensive. And I think at one time, there really were only expensive hairpieces.

But now this has become so common. Men have stopped worrying about the stigma of having a hairpiece and want a natural solution. So have women who have lost their hair (and there are a lot of women out there losing hair).

Hair pieces (or hair systems) have improved so much and look so much more natural, if not completely natural now. You will be amazed at how natural a hairline and feel you can get now.

The way I used to look at it when I first started to wear a hairpiece (in my pre-transition days), I am going to get made fun of for being bald (for some reason, it is still socially acceptable to make fun of bald people and ridicule them, even though it truly is very humiliating), so I may as well do something that makes me feel good. I may be made fun of, but I will be made fun of while having hair! The bottom line here is, making yourself feel good.

Back to where to get this hair. There are a couple of places I have found which are very good for hair replacement. By the way, this is good whether you are still living as a man and want to have hair then, or you are ready to live as a female. These places do both men's and women's hair systems.

There is a distinct advantage to losing your hair. You can have whatever style, color and length of hair you want – INSTANTLY. So see. There is always a gift in everything! My hair looks way better than it ever would have if I had kept my hair and let it grow out. I would imagine it would have been a frizzy mess all the time!

The two places I have found are Toplace.com and Coolpiece.com. They both are very reasonable, and you can order online. You do not even have to leave your house. It does not get more private than that!

Now, you do have to make your own impression of your head. Do NOT be intimidated by this as I was. These hair places have got us all intimidated into believing this is a horribly complicated process and an art form we could not understand.

Pooey on that. You CAN do this yourself.

IF you have an existing hair system, you can even mail that into them and they will make a copy. Very simple. And you will save thousands over what you are paying now. I pay less now for a completely new system than I used to pay for REPAIRS on my old systems. Seriously!

If you are not currently wearing a hair system, they have great instructions on their respective web sites on how to make an impression for them to create your system, so I will leave that to the experts. But just realize, it is not that hard, and requires no special tools. Just some handiwrap, tape, and a marker basically.

You will also have to make some specifications when ordering the system. Here are some specifications I would use:

1) Density – Go 100% all over except in the front hairline. Go 85-90%, or you could even go a little lower. You WANT to see scalp. This makes it look natural. Look at women's hair. You can see scalp. This is what makes it look natural. Do NOT go any higher than 100% or it might look fake, plus it will be very hard to style. You can even go a little lower than 100%. I know we all are paranoid of seeing scalp and wanting thick hair, but trust me, 80-100% is VERY thick. If you want to get a "man's" one while you are at it (if you are not living as a female), go much less on the density. Around 60-70%. They have pictures on their web sites for you to do some comparisons on what density you want.
2) Do a poly border around the edge, except in the front. This will allow you to tape the system down and then glue in the front.
3) Pick a base color that is close to your own scalp. They have this explained on their web sites, and you know what is best for you.
4) If you like curls, get one with curls already in it. The less you can style it, the better for the hair, and the less work for you. Otherwise, get it straight. You can always curl it when you want. I have never been able to get the hair perfectly straight, so just realize that. Unless it is Asian

hair (which is just naturally bone straight), it will probably have a little wave in it. This is NATURAL. Most people's hair has a little wave in it when it is longer.
5) Get the hair an inch or two longer than you want it to allow for evening out around the edges. Also, realize it will be longer in the back then the front. SO when picking the length, determine how far you want it to come down in the front. That is your minimum length. About 12-14 inches will bring it a little below your shoulders.
6) If your hair on the sides and back is thick and full and grows fine, go with a partial hair system. However, if it is thinner or grows slowly (as most men's does), then go with a full cap system. Leave a little room in the corners and the back for your own hair to show, but other than that, go full. It will just look more natural.

Now when you get your hair, you will need to get it cut. You have already decided on a hairstyle. You can take your picture off the hairstyler.com, if you found one you like. Or take one out of a magazine. Or if you have a picture of yourself in a wig or old hairpiece with a style you liked, take that in. Then call around to some wig places. They can help you with that. Hair Direct can cut it for you if you order from them. That is another option. I have not used them personally, but I have read good things. Check out their web site, if you are worried about finding a place to get your hair cut. Most wig and hair replacement places should be able to help you out. The hair replacement places might charge more since it is not one of their systems. Just call around and compare prices and who you feel comfortable with.

Remember, lots of women lose their hair (chemotherapy, alopecia, heredity, etc), so there are plenty of places who will be able to cut your hair.

Once you have it cut, you are ready to go.

So I hope all this was a help. If you have lost your hair and follow my advice for a permanent hair solution, you will save yourself thousands and thousands of dollars and, frankly, have a better hair system. These things need to be replaced every 6-12 months, so it is great to have a cost effective solution that looks so NATURAL.

And do not rule out wigs if you do not want to mess with a hairpiece. Just do not be afraid to spend a little more to get a more natural looking wig. You will still spend way less than going with the expensive hair replacement places.

Hair Removal

Hair removal is one of the most important parts of your transition for passability. In fact, in my opinion this is THE most important step for passability. More important than makeup, hair, body, clothes. I have seen many girls get makeup and clothes, get on hormones, even have surgeries and not do one bit of hair removal. This is a big mistake. Because if you have a beard, it is going to be really hard to pass as female (at least as well as you could).

It is hard to completely cover up a beard, even if you shave closely (which you will need to do prior to putting on makeup). Besides, what if you meet somebody you like and he or she touches your cheek and feels stubble! Eek! It is not the end of the world, though. Do not worry. And if this person gets freaked out by a little stubble, then that is their problem. However, we do want to aim for as feminine as possible.

Now, if you really do not want to transition, but you do want to go out and dress sometimes or something of that nature, you can just go to the part about temporary hair removal later in this section. Perhaps you are married and like being a man with a feminine side at times, and do not want to get rid of your beard. That is ok too. Remember, we are all unique individuals. Whoever you are is ok, and there is no judgment here. Just read about temporary hair removal and use a good full coverage foundation. There is good makeup to cover a beard. Just do a real close shave and use Max Factor Pan -Cake or another full coverage foundation to cover up, and you will be good to go for a night out. See the Makeup section for more information.

Also, you might not really care if you are passable. Some do not, and you know what, I think that is very cool. Just be who you are and who cares what anybody thinks. It may not even be about looking exactly like a woman for you. It is all good. This is about being you.

However, many of you may be very concerned with passability (which if you are going to live full time you need to be) and/or just want to be smooth. You will want to read this whole section. If you are planning to transition to any degree, you really need to remove the hair on your face at least, in some way.

Temporary Hair Removal

As I said, this section is for quick hair removal, for removing hair until you can get it removed permanently, or if you just do not want to remove hair permanently.

The first way and obvious way of removing hair is shaving. You need to do a very close shave prior to putting makeup on. If you have a heavy beard, you might need to shave twice a day. Do not skip this step ever if you are going out. It may sound obvious, but I have seen some girls with a beard, so I am putting this in here just in case.

You will also want to shave your body, depending on what you want to show and who will be seeing you. If you are not ready or do not want to shave your whole body, you can get away with just shaving your legs usually. There are a lot of long sleeved, high necked sexy and pretty dresses out there that are perfect for you at this stage. In fact, go with a long skirt or some nice pants if you do not want to shave your legs.

I like the Schick Extreme 3 Razor, either for women or for sensitive skin. Your leg skin may break out a bit at first, especially if you have sensitive skin. It is not used to being shaved all the time, and I have found this to be the best razor for giving you a smooth shave and not irritating your skin. However, no matter what razor you use, your skin will settle down over time as it gets used to being shaved more. Just like when you first started having to shave your face.

You can also use this to shave the rest of your body. Some girls do a full body shave every day. Only you know your situation and the clothes you are wearing. If you are part time or just want to go out dressed, there is obviously no need to shave your whole body every day. Just do not skip shaving any body parts that will be showing, including the hands.

The next temporary hair removal that lasts a little longer is a depilatory. This is a cream you rub on your skin that removes the hair from the skin. It will typically remove the hair lower down from the surface than shaving will so your skin will stay smoother longer. Nair is a well known depilatory. I have not had good luck with these. It never seems to completely remove the hair, and it irritates my skin (but I have sensitive skin). But it may work great for you. Try it once to see how it works for you, if this interests you. Just make sure you follow the instructions. You do not want to leave it on too long or you will really hurt your skin. I think too, our hair is more coarse then a genetic female's hair, so it does not work as well as it does on a genetic female's hair, in my opinion. But give it a try, as I said, if this interests you. I know a lot of TS women that love Nair and others depilatories such as Veet.

Semi-Permanent Hair Removal (Waxing)

Waxing is a great way to remove the hair for weeks at a time. There is a little more work and pain involved, but it is a great way to remove hair. You can go to places to have it done. Many spas do this. Look in the yellow pages under hair removal. Nail places do it sometimes (at least on the eyebrows).

If you are worried somebody will wonder why you are doing this, do not worry. Chances are nobody will ask. Besides which, men get hair removed all the time. They like to be smooth too.

Especially if they work out – they want to show off their muscles. So do not worry about it.

You can also buy waxing kits at the drugstore. It is really not that hard, and it is cheaper as well. That way you can do it in the privacy of your own home.

You can either spread the wax on the area you want to remove the hair from and then pull it off with strips they provide (and rip the hair out) or you can use pre-waxed strips. Those are great. All you do is peal them apart, place them on your skin, rub to get them warm and attached to the hair, and then pull. Not all of these kits are created equal, so you might have to try a couple to find one that works well for you.

It does sting a bit. I will not lie to you about that. But at least it is quick – kind of like ripping a really strong band-aid off a hairy area. Feel free to say a couple good swear words or scream the first time.

It is worth it though. You will be amazed at the results.

Also, the more times you do it, the less it will hurt. Plus, you will build up a tolerance for pain. It will not even phase you after a bit.

I wax my arms and my eyebrows. Now my arms were the hairiest part of my body. I am not kidding. I think I could have braided it. It was just awful.

So I decided I was going to wax my arms. Remember, I had nobody to talk to about this or give me advice. So I went and bought a waxing kit. I spread some of the wax on my arm. Then put the strip on. And started to pull. I thought I was going to die. No lie. Boy did that hurt. I had so much hair on my arms for one thing. Plus it was my first time. At this point, though, I had already cleared that first strip of hair off, so I kind of had to finish or have to think up an explanation quick for this strange rectangle sized hair-free area on the top of my left arm.

But I toughed it out. I wanted my arms clear. Each time I pulled was just agony, and in general I was a big baby. Then I learned not to wait to pull. Put it on and rip. Do not sit there trying to work up the courage or it just seems worse. Just like ripping a bandage off.

Just grit your teeth and bare it if you have a similar experience. It will hurt less and less.

The reasons for this are as follows:

1) Your hair will grow back in finer and thinner, so it will be easier to pull out next time. This is a nice benefit of waxing.
2) You have four cycles of hair growth. The first time you wax, you have 4 growth cycles of hair on your arm. The next time you wax, you will only have one cycle's worth of hair.
3) You develop a higher tolerance for pain the more you do it and it honestly does not hurt as much.

One disadvantage of waxing is you do have to let your hair grow out a bit so there is enough hair for the wax and strips to grip onto. You usually need about 1/8" to ¼" in length. I usually have to let my hair grow out a week at least before waxing. So just keep this in mind when deciding where you want to wax, as you will have to let the hair grow out a bit (and may or may not want to cover up the affected area).

One area I would definitely recommend waxing is your eyebrows. That way you will not have to constantly be plucking them. Plucking is slow torture in my book. Waxing hurts, but it is one rip and you are done. And it lasts longer than plucking. This will give you some facial feminization too. You can arch your eyebrows like a woman's. Women tend to have higher, more arched eyebrows. Something like a slight surprised look (with the eyebrows that is). Just realize if you do wax your eyebrows, people will notice. So do this when you are ready and want to do some feminizing of your face. It can be tricky since you have to shape your brows, so I would recommend going somewhere to do this, at least the first time, but you can do it at home. I do it at home, and it is not that bad. Just be careful you do not take off too much hair and shape them as you would like. Making your eyebrows too thin or having no eyebrows at all (I have seen this) is not a natural look. Although you can always pencil them back in, so it is not the end of the world.

You can also pluck your eyebrows if you would prefer. Get a good set of tweezers. You can find these in the women's makeup section usually of most drugstores. Plucking can be good as you can go slowly and shape your eyebrows as little or as much as you like more easily than with waxing. It just does take longer and is more painful in the long run, in my opinion.

Permanent Hair Removal

If you plan on transitioning to the point of living full time as a woman, you are going to want to remove hair permanently. If you do go on hormones (read the Hormones section for guidance on this. You may choose to not do hormones), a lot of body hair will actually naturally fall out or become finer. However, the hormones will not help so much with facial hair unfortunately, which is the most important area to clear the hair from. As I have said before, it is hard to cover up a beard completely. Having a clear face is more important to your passability than any other thing, and TS women often neglect that, getting caught up in clothes and makeup and hair and surgeries and forgetting they have a beard. Hair removal takes some time, so you want to start this AS SOON AS POSSIBLE if you plan on going full time. Start on your FACE first. This is very important.

There are two methods of permanent hair removal: electrolysis and laser. Both are very good.

Electrolysis is the oldest way of removing hair and is guaranteed to be permanent. It is a very effective way of removing hair but takes a very long time as each hair is treated individually and may take several treatments to totally kill. Electrolysis also is quite painful as a needle is stuck in each hair and an electric current sent into the follicle to kill it. It is not the needle that hurts but the chemical reaction in the hair when the current is sent in. But it does hurt, to varying degrees.

Laser is a WAY quicker and much less painful method of removing hair, but not guaranteed to be permanent. However, it is pretty darn permanent.

In any case, with laser they can clear your whole face in 15-30 minutes, whereas at the beginning your electrologist can probably cover about a square inch or two in that time period. However, once again laser is not guaranteed to be permanent, but from my experience, it is fairly permanent, and can give you quicker clearance. More details later in this section.

The best way to clear hair is by a combination of laser and electrolysis. Laser to do an initial clearing, and then electrolysis for cleanup or to work on hairs the laser does not work on (i.e. blonde, grey and white hairs).

As I have said, electrolysis is a very effective process that does kill the hairs. The problem is, a needle has to be stuck into each hair follicle and then an electric current is shot in to kill the follicle.

Some (not all) hairs can take up to 8-10 times to kill. It can also be pretty painful, depending on the method they use.

I had a very good electrologist and she used different methods on me. When we were first treating the hair, it was much coarser and thicker, so she would stick a needle in each follicle and then shoot the current in and hold it for about 5-10 seconds. This was EXTREMELY painful. However, it was the method she found that worked best on my hair. Make sure your electrologist is willing to try different methods at first to see what works best on your hair.

They do have topicals to numb the pain, so do not fear completely. And it is worth it. It really does kill the hair. But it can take awhile to clear your face obviously.

I did this little weekly torture session over and over, an hour a week, for almost 2 years. My hair became finer and less coarse. Then she was able to switch to a different method that hurt less and was much quicker since my hair was finer. Just quick little shots, like a little zap. After what I had been through, that was nothing. Your pain tolerance definitely increases while you go through this. So take heart in that as well. If anybody doubts a transsexual's determination, they should try getting electrolysis on their upper lip and then they will know, this is not just a whim!

My electrolysis cost $60 each week, and that was a deal, at least in Chicago. Obviously, this can get quite expensive, but it is worth it. And it gives you a sense of accomplishment. It is a solid, needed step you are constantly taking towards your goal of being the woman you are. So that is a mental benefit of it. Plus you do not need to tell anybody. Especially with electrolysis, it will not be that noticeable for awhile. And if they do notice, just say you are sick of shaving. Plenty of men get laser anymore just because they do not want to shave or have the irritation to their skin. The same reasoning can apply to electrolysis.

Electrolysis is still a great option as it will work on any type of hair on any skin type (unlike laser which works best on certain hair colors and skin tones). It is also great for cleaning up a few spare hairs. And as I have said, it is definitely permanent. So do not discount electrolysis. The pain does become easier and it will work on whatever hair you have. And you can do as little or much as you like. It is also cheaper than laser at first (not in the long run), so if your budget is a bit more limited you can do that and at least be taking some permanent hair removal steps.

Now, if I have horrified you with my electrolysis tales, take heart. First off, remember the wonderful benefits of electrolysis. But more importantly, there is another wonderful option for permanent hair removal now. It is laser. People have varying opinions on this, especially electrologists. They are still not allowed to call it permanent, but this has improved a lot since I first started transitioning in 2000.

A laser removes hair very quickly and relatively painlessly. It works by being attracted to the pigment in your hair. For this reason, it works best on dark hair, and the BEST on people with dark hair and light skin, but not just on those combinations. However, there have been many improvements in lasers over the years. It does not work on grey, white, or blonde hairs (although they are finding a way to possibly work on blonde hair from what my laser person tells me), since hairs of these colors do not have the pigment necessary for the laser.

Now, if you are like me, you have dark hair and light hairs. Maybe some grey mixed in with the dark or blonde mixed in with the dark. What you can do is start with the laser. This will remove the dark hairs. Do this for about 6-12 months and then do electrolysis on the light hairs. And there will always be stray stubborn hairs that refuse to be removed by laser, so you can get these zapped with electrolysis. Or you may have so few, you can just quick run a razor over these when you wash your face in the morning, if they bother you

Let me take a quick break for a side note here. Do not become so paranoid about hair that you cannot stand to have ONE hair on your face or body. You will drive yourself crazy. It is pretty hard, if not impossible, to remove EVERY hair. Besides which, new hairs are always popping up. It does not mean you are not a woman if you have some hairs in unwanted places or that anybody will notice. With laser and electrolysis you can get the hair fine enough and thin enough where nobody will notice. Remember, we are always more critical of ourselves than other people are. Also remember, genetic women get a lot of unwanted hair too. Welcome to the club of unwanted hair!!!!!! And having to shave your face or your chest or whatever does not make you a man. I used to feel self conscious about this. Understandably so. It is just another "outside thing" that has no bearing on your femaleness, however.

Now back to our regularly scheduled permanent hair removal story.

Laser is more expensive than electrolysis at the beginning. But in the long run, it is cheaper. And you can clear your face much quicker. Remember, start with your face.

Laser is much more comfortable than electrolysis. It kind of feels like somebody is snapping a red hot rubber band on your face again and again, but it is quick and nowhere near the pain of electrolysis. Plus, in 20-30 minutes you can have a clear face (for this treatment at least). How cool is that?!

Where can you find electrologists and laser places? They are everywhere. Hair removal is a huge business. Look in the yellow pages under hair removal, or even laser or electrologists. You can do a search online as well. Just type in "electrologists" or "laser" or "hair removal" and your area.

Once again, do not worry about looking funny going in or what they will think. Plenty of men get hair removed now. They want to be smooth too or not have to hassle with shaving or deal with the red bumps underneath their chin. Besides, you are a PAYING client. They are more than happy and appreciative to have a paying customer, believe me. So walk in and be proud! If they give you a hard time at all, find another place that treats you right. There are plenty out there.

A summary of Hair Removal Methods and their advantages and disadvantages is given on the next page.

Method	Advantages	Disadvantages
Shaving	Immediate Quick Cheap Temporary if you don't want to remove hair permanently Painless	Can irritate Skin Not permanent
Depilatories	Immediate Quick Lasts longer than shaving	May irritate skin Only lasts a few days
Waxing	Long Results (6-8 Weeks) Quick Immediate Relatively Cheap	Not permanent Ingrown hairs are more common Can be a little painful Have to grow hair out more beforehand
Electrolysis	Permanent (only guaranteed permanent method) Works on any type or color of hair Great for small areas or cleanup of spare hairs	Takes a long time Very painful Expensive Can irritate skin Can only clear a small area at a time
Laser	Permanent or Close to permanent Quick Can clear large areas in one treatment	Can be a little painful Expensive at first, but cheaper in the long run than electrolysis Does not work at all or well on all hair colors or skin tones (not good for blonde, grey or white hairs)

Summary of Hair Removal Methods

Hormones

This section is something that I think every TG needs to read. Hormones are like this right of passage in the TS community. They are used to feminize your body and face some. Everyone wants to know if you are on them. They are required in the Harry Benjamin standards for transitioning. Many of us go to a therapist in order to get on them. As I said, it seems to be the right of passage into "being a female". It seems to "legitimize" you in the community.

Before I get into the details of this section, I would like to emphasize to only take hormones under a doctor's care and after going through therapy and receiving a letter of recommendation to go on hormones. These are serious drugs and not something to be taken on a whim, and you want to take them safely.

I would also like to point out that while there are many great benefits to taking hormones (softer skin, body hair loss, curvier body, a more feminine appearance), they do not MAKE you a woman. Let me repeat that. Drugs do NOT make you a woman. They do not legitimize you. You do not need them to be a woman. You already ARE a woman. Remember that. You do not need a fake substance to make you a woman.

There are three main types of drugs you can take. They are as follows:

1) Estrogen – This is the main female hormone for feminizing the body. This can be taken via an injection, orally, or a patch. A patch is the best and safest method, in my opinion..
2) Progesterone – Usually taken with estrogen and promotes breast growth

3) Testosterone blocker – This is to help the estrogen be more effective and block testosterone's effects on your body. Spironolactone is the most popular of these.

Hormones do have some nice benefits I realize many TS's are seeking. Some of these benefits include:

1) Breast growth
2) Curvier, more feminine body (bigger hips, backside)
3) Softer skin
4) Loss or reduction of body hair
5) A more feminine look to your face

Every person reacts to them differently, so your may experience varying degrees of the above. Many girls also report feeling more feminine and at peace.

Some side effects that you may also experience, which are good or bad, depending on your opinion:

1) Decreased sex drive
2) Loss of some muscle
3) You may be more emotional
4) Depression at times
5) Your nipples may hurt or be a bit tender at times
6) Sterility after taking the hormones long enough (you do not have to worry about this for the first 6 months usually) – so be sure you do not want to have any more children prior to going on hormones.
7) Inability to achieve an erection (sometimes)
8) There is a risk of blood clots, which can be fatal.

I am not trying to scare you with any of this. Only to educate you so you will know what you are getting into. Yes, there are benefits to going on hormones. There are also risks and things to be considered. Being under a proper doctor's and therapist's care will help you to manage these risks better.

You may also feel perfectly female now and have a very feminine look and not want to go on hormones. Or you may not like to take drugs. Talk this over with your therapist. I believe too much emphasis is put on taking hormones to become a woman and it puts a lot of TS women at risk. It should be a personal decision to go on hormones – not a requirement.

Here are some guidelines to follow when considering going on hormones and once you are on them:

1) Do not go on hormones lightly. This is a serious move. You will be changing your body. They have some permanent affects on your body (e.g sterility over time, breast growth) that you need to make sure you are ok with before going on them. In other words, be sure this is for you and you are ready.
2) Do NOT self medicate. These are serious drugs with potentially serious risks. Take them under a doctor's care. Make sure you have seen a therapist for at least 2 months prior to going on hormones and have received a letter from them saying you are ready for hormones.
3) Use a patch for taking the hormones, if possible. If you go on estrogen, ask if you can use a patch. I think this is the best option. It will give you the estrogen in a low dosage over time rather than all at once like an oral or injection does. The patch is a much more natural way to receive the hormones and is MUCH safer than any other method of taking the hormones, in my opinion. Avoid oral hormones, in my opinion, altogether.
4) Value yourself and your health more than being on hormones. Do not ever do ANYTHING in your transition, especially hormones, at the expense of your health. You can transition healthily. You can be on

hormones safely and protect your health. Your health is not something to be taken for granted or lightly disregarded for "the cause" of your transition. To put it bluntly, you will not enjoy being a woman if you are sick or even dead.

5) Take responsibility for your health. Do not leave it all up to the doctor. He has hundreds of patients. Make him answer any questions you ever have. If you are suffering any bad pains or other symptoms, ask the doctor about them and MAKE HIM ANSWER to your satisfaction. Push it all you want.

6) Do not be intimidated by the doctor. You are their patient. You are paying them. They owe you answers to your questions. If they get mad or do not want to answer your questions or investigate your concerns, find another doctor.

7) If you feel continuing pains in your chest, demand an X-ray. Period. Better safe than sorry. These may be an indication of blood clots.

8) As your hormone levels change, you might start to feel more emotional. If you find yourself becoming deeply depressed and think it is related to the hormones, reduce the dosage or even go off the hormones before going on an anti-depressant. It is not worth being depressed all the time.

As I have said before, there are risks to taking hormones. I would like to relate my own personal experience with hormones to relate these more to you.

Before I tell this story, I want to make clear, I understand why girls go on hormones. They do have feminizing effects on the body. Many of these can be achieved in other ways, though. I am not telling you NOT to go on them (although I would personally not recommend them anymore). That is a personal decision.

However, I am telling you that you need to do this very carefully, and you must learn to take control of your health when you do and not rely on your therapist or doctor to watch out for you.

I will also relate my experience with hormones so you can make an educated decision about going on them (because you do not HAVE to go on them if you do not want to) and if you do, to do it more wisely and safely than I did.

Like most TS women starting their transition, I was very determined to get on hormones. I did not ever feel like I needed them to be a woman, but I did feel the need to legitimize myself somehow and have the experience and follow the rules all the other TS's were following in their transition. I was excited to see the benefits they would have on my body (mainly breasts and more curves). After diligently going to my therapist for over 2 months, I received my letter to go on hormones.

There were a few doctors in my area, but one was closest, so I picked him. What is odd is I had gone to this doctor a couple years before for another problem I had had (he was an urologist) and he was horrible then. No bedside manner. Creepy looking. Messy, dirty office. No privacy consideration. He literally explained my condition in front of another patient. Really disrespectful and unprofessional type of behavior from a doctor. I really did not like him.

However, he was convenient. Wrong criteria (at least the sole criteria) for picking your doctor.

Make a note of that. Convenience is not the most important factor when choosing your hormone doctor. You need to find someone you feel comfortable with and who is professional and respectful and cares about doing his job as well as making money. So if the first doctor you like is unprofessional or makes you uncomfortable somehow or you just do not feel he or she is watching out for your health properly, then go find another doctor. Your therapist can point you to other doctors in your area.

A quick and important caution. I know I have said this before, but DO NOT SELF MEDICATE. This is very tempting. You can buy hormones (possibly illegally) over the internet. The problem is, you will not be monitoring your blood levels or you might be taking the wrong dosages for you, and you could literally KILL yourself. This is not worth your life. Your health is the most important thing and you can take hormones and care for your health. Read on to find out more.

There is a lot of money to be made in the TS community and some doctors realize that. You are a money-maker for them and you are motivated to take steps towards your transition.

Many of us have this view of doctors as special beings to be respected and revered and not questioned. They are not God, though. They are business people just like every other place you go to give your money. And they want your money. Remember that. You are their customer. Expect to get treated correctly.

I am not saying these doctors are all bad. There are great doctors out there. Many of them do want to help and do care about your health. But they are doctors with a business to run. So just be careful.

Doctors are also very busy. They see a lot of patients every day, going from patient room to patient room. You cannot be the only person they are monitoring and worrying about, so you have to take some responsibility for your health and being firm with the doctor with any questions or concerns you have. This is another mistake I made as you will see later. And doctors are human. They can get distracted or make mistakes too.

Anyway, back to my story. I excitedly made my appointment to see this doctor. I went in to seem him for my initial visit. I was still part time, but I went in as my female self. He did a brief checkup on me, but his biggest point he seemed to want to make to me was that he knew how to bill the insurance companies so it would get paid and nobody would get in trouble. Another warning sign there. His biggest point should have been how he knew how to keep me healthy.

He also told me he had been doing this for over 30 years. He was one of the original doctors to work with TS's. SO I was going on his experience alone. How could he be bad if he had worked that long right?

We also have this thing when we are starting out that we are just so grateful to anybody who is nice to us or treats us respectfully as our female self. Well they damn well should! We are human beings, worthy of respect and dignity and proper care like everybody else, not worms in the dust groveling for any sign of politeness or respect. Remember that.

I went for my blood test. Everything turned out ok.

I went on weekly estrogen injections, Progesterone, plus I was on Premarin (an orally taken estrogen drug) and Spironolactone (a testosterone blocker).

For the record, I never really felt any different, but then again, I was not looking to feel any different. I already felt like a woman and feminine. Many will say they felt an immediate difference once they went on estrogen. Could be. I am not them. But they may just be feeling what they want or perhaps it does legitimately change how they feel. I believe the sense of calm and peace they feel comes from that they are finally doing what they want with their lives more than the drug itself, but that is just my opinion.

They feel how they feel, and I respect that and accept what they are saying. Every person is different and nobody is wrong.

Anyway, I dutifully did the weekly injections and took my pills. After about 5 months, I started to get some pains in my chest. At first I thought I pulled a muscle. Then I thought maybe I had bronchitis since it seemed to be in my lung area. I never made the connection with the hormones.

Now, this doctor never came in to see me when I went for my weekly injections. He was there, but he would send his Physician's assistant (PA) or nurse in. The only thing he did was sign the paper for the insurance. This was bad. I should not have let that happen. But I did not want to cause waves. Meanwhile, he is charging me around $80 a visit for simply giving me an injection (and I provided the injection myself, per his prescription). I was not getting much for my money.

Once again, I am telling you this story so you can learn from my mistakes. Make your doctor see you and talk to you each time you go in to his or her office, even if it is just for an injection.

So these pains are getting worse, and I mention them to the PA. I figure I am in a doctor's office, I may as well ask even if it "didn't have anything to do with the hormones" (or so I thought). He said, "It is probably just pleurisy."

The pains would come and go. I asked the PA a couple more times. "Oh, it is just pleurisy or something".

I still never pushed it. I hated to complain. I had this phobia of being a hypochondriac. And I hated pushing things. Like I did not want to whine or be a nag.

Plus, I was in a doctor's care, right? Surely they would act more concerned if it was something serious or concerned them after I (rather apologetically) mentioned it to them.

Then around 6 months into my hormone treatment I started getting sharper pains. I finally went online and looked up what pleurisy was. It did sound like I had that. However never self-diagnose yourself. Whatever you THINK you have, you can find proof on the internet that you do. Plus, different conditions can have the same symptoms.

ASK THE DOCTOR. MAKE HIM INVESTIGATE IT. DO NOT LET THEM BLOW YOU OFF. Even if you think you are being a hypochondriac, who cares. You have the right to ask. This is your health you are dealing with! Your most precious gift.

Little did I know what was cooking inside of me.

I also had a bad habit of putting off the doctor when I was sick or had a pain figuring things would go away, and they usually did. This one would too, I figured.

This one did not.

Month 7. President's day weekend in fact. Sunday night, I had horrible pains. Kept me up for awhile in fact, but I finally got to sleep.

I kind of shrugged it off. I was not ready to go to the doctor. Seemed like a waste of time. It would probably go away. You cannot run to the doctor every time you get a pain, right?

Monday night, it hit. The worst pain I have ever had in my life. I spent the whole night up. I could not lay down or the pain would get worse. It was so bad, it kept convulsing my body so I kept bending over. Believe it or not, I still was not scared. I thought I had one VERY bad case of bronchitis of pneumonia or pleurisy. But I was really in pain. Just horrible. I cannot even describe. But I was always proud of my ability to grin and bare it, so I waited until morning to do something.

So in the morning, I drove myself over to the Immediate care Facility. They nonchalantly put me in a room. No sense of urgency, and frankly, I did not have one either. I was just in pain and wanted some medicine to clear up what I thought was severe bronchitis or pneumonia.

They took some X-rays and I had a huge blood clot in both lungs. These had obviously been in there since at least 2 months before.

All these clots had to do was break off and go to my brain or heart and I was dead. Scary huh? So they show me the X-ray, but they tell me rather calmly and matter of factly. Not like it is that big a deal (probably to keep me from freaking out). However I am starting to finally get a LITTLE scared, as I have heard a bit about blood clots. I was definitely still in my stupidly brave stage, shrugging things off.

So I call my sister (80 miles away) and say I am going to have to go to the hospital. So I drive myself there. Once again, this was serious. Why did they let me do that, I do not know. So I drive over, and they send me for a Catscan. This was excruciating as I had to lie in that thing while still trying to keep my body convulsing from the pain and the technician telling me, you have to lay still dear. I was about ready to slap her!

Then I waited. And waited. For 2 hours. Our hospitals are crazy. No wonder they get sued. They already knew I had this blood clot that could break off and they let me sit. Finally, they call me up and tell me I have to stay overnight. I reply, "I can't stay overnight. I have a dog! Can I go home first and take care of her?" "No, you can't leave the hospital." Great.

They still have not told me how serious this is. So I go to check in, and they are being very businesslike and professional and inform me I am going into intensive care. Finally I started to cry. Enough of being calm.

I said, could somebody PLEASE tell me what EXACTLY is wrong with me. Do I have a tumor or something? Why am I being checked into Intensive Care?????? That sounds pretty darn serious! SO they told me, I had a huge blood clot in both lungs and it was life threatening.

So I call my sister (on a cell phone that is almost dying, the hospital wouldn't let me use their phone of course). And I get rolled up into Intensive Care, all by my little self.

The whole thing was surreal. After that they took really good care of me, I must say. The nurses were just wonderful. Did not blink an eye about me being a TS. Most people I have encountered in the medical profession have been very professional to me, for the record. It is only my hormone doctor, who should have been the best, who was a jerk. So do not be afraid of being mistreated by medical people. For the most part they are very professional and respectful and do their job.

I was in the hospital eight days with an IV and on Coumadin to thin my blood for a year. Very scary, but I made it out alive and healthy, and that is what counts.

As I sat there in that hospital room alone, though, it really gave me time to think. That was a pretty scary incident looking back on it, but at the time, I did not see it that way. I just cried a lot as those hormones exited my body (I could not be on them anymore since the clots were caused by the estrogen). Anybody called me and I was weepy. I feel pretty sorry for anybody who called me as I cried their ear off! I think it was a combination of the hormones balancing out in my body and just being sad I had to go off them that made me so weepy

But I sat there thinking, what does this mean? Can I still transition? Can I get SRS? Of course, I probably should have been a bit worried about clots coming back and killing me. You can see where my head was. As it is for many TS's. We get so focused on our goal of transitioning, we forget about other things, like our health.

But I came out healthy. Per the hematologist, I could not take hormones anymore. It was too risky. I agreed.

Meanwhile, I am still thinking. I have not been taking very good care of my health. I was about 34 at the time, and like most young people, I took my health for granted. All of a sudden, I think, boy, I need to start taking care of myself. This transition is not worth my health or dying for.

So I started to eat better. Did some research and found out more about blood clotting risks. I am not the only girl by far to have had this problem.

Hormones were not the right choice for me. I felt perfectly female beforehand and never felt a burning need to be on them other than a need to follow the Harry Benjamin rules and somehow legitimize myself. That was my personal experience. For other people, hormones may be a good choice.

Follow the lessons I learned in my hormone experience so you can make the right choice for yourself and if you do choose to go on hormones, do it wisely and safely.

I would only go on hormones if you are very masculine looking and would benefit from the feminizing effects of hormones and have received a letter of recommendation from a gender therapist. Also, do this under an appropriate doctor's care.

You are a special person. Take care of your health while you take hormones.

Picturing Yourself

How do you see yourself? How would you like to look? What would you like to do? Be part time, full time, post operative, on stage, married to a woman or a man, living where, doing what kind of work. How would people treat you? What kinds of friends would you like to have? What color would your hair be? How would you dress?

Write all this out. Write it out just as you have always dreamed living. Put all the juicy details in. Nobody will read this but you. It's just between you and the Universe. This is your fantasy. What you want to be, do, have.

Now put this some place safe just for you. Read it at least once a day for at least 21 days. This will help you begin to really develop a mindset of who you are. You will become that person in your head.

Play with it too. Rewrite is. Your tastes may change.

Self image is very important in your transition. How you think of yourself will draw you to what you want. I felt totally female in my transition. I just KNEW what I was inside, how I had always felt.

I realize not everybody has that, but you can acquire it by picturing yourself this way. Just do not convince yourself if you do not want to be a woman. That is ok too! In other words, if you just want to dress up sometimes or whatever, that is fine too. Just picture yourself like that. The bottom line is clarifying what you want and picturing it in your head. You can experience things before they happen this way as well and might find something is not for you.

When you start thinking of yourself as female, your body starts to correspond. Trust me, this works. Think a happy thought. What happens to your face? It reflects that thought. Your face softens, you might grin or smile. Think how you want to tell someone off, and your face will change too. You will frown or tense up.

The same thing happens as you think of yourself as female. Your face will hold a more "female" expression. It will be softer, gentler. Think softer, gentler. Watch your face. As you walk, you will begin to walk more gently, with a more female grace. The way you eat. The way you sit down. All of these will begin to become more feminine.

You have to BREATHE being a female if you eventually want to be a female on the outside. It is who you are. Having this mindset that you ARE a female will make your transition happen much more naturally.

These little subtle changes that happen are what truly makes you passable and also help you become the woman you want to be.

Voice

Voice is an area that is sometimes overlooked. However, it is an area you want to work on to make it as female-sounding as possible.

Voice is one of those areas that can "give you away", but it is also important to become comfortable with your voice and not worry about it being "perfect". You do not want to obsess about it to the point where you are miserable if it is not "perfectly female". Remember, love and appreciate your uniqueness.

Getting your voice somewhere that you like takes practice. It usually does not happen overnight. The better an impersonator of other people you are, the easier it will be for you to develop a female voice as you can "imitate" easily how women talk. Once again, listen to women. Imitate how they talk when you are by yourself. Practice. Tape yourself. Listen to how you sound and then make changes of things you do not like.

A good voice may take awhile to develop to your satisfaction. I still work on mine sometimes! It is constantly evolving.

What is nice is it is something you can practice anytime you want - while you are driving the car, getting ready in the morning, walking the dog, in the bathroom (at home, might raise some eyebrows in public). Get into this habit of practicing talking and listening to yourself.

I do want to just briefly state a little bit about learning to love your voice and not becoming paranoid about it (as I did).

The first thing to realize, as with looks, is women have all different types of voices. High, deep, medium, monotone, sexy, masculine (yes some do), feminine. So do not worry that your voice has to be this perfect female voice to be good.

Also, do not get worried if somebody calls you Sir on the phone or whatever. First off, they might just be a jerk, so that is their problem, not yours. But second, even genetic women get called "Sir" sometimes on the phone. And their voices do not necessarily have to be super low. So just do not let it bother you or you will actually attract more attention to your voice. If you are self conscious of your voice, other people will be more conscious of it.

This was one of my BIGGEST challenges in my transition and self acceptance. I think it went right along with being OK with who I was. I had and have a very feminine voice. It was not male. But it was not exactly totally female either. It was a transgendered woman's voice. Well, guess what. I AM A TRANSGENDERED WOMAN. So I guess that makes sense. But of course, I wanted a perfect female voice.

However, a perfect female voice can be tricky to achieve. This is due to the fact that our voice boxes develop differently. Our voice boxes are bigger than a genetic woman's. Thus, a genetic female's voice simply has a different resonance, frequency, etc than a genetic male's voice box.

Well, we cannot exactly change that. So what we cannot change, we should embrace.

However, we can make our voice sound really good and pretty darn female.

Now, as I have said, I was very self conscious of my voice. Anytime anybody called me "Sir" or "he" on the phone was an agony. I hated my voice. I tried and tried so hard. People who knew me before seemed to go out of their way to tell me my voice gave me away (people are so helpful sometimes aren't they).

I would like to make a quick note about how differently people hear you, though, depending on whether they knew you pre-transition or not.

People who knew you before (and this includes you yourself by the way), associate the sound of your voice with the "old" you. Consequently they think of it as male.

Well what I noticed was, people who did not know me before thought I had a great voice, a feminine voice, a nice voice. I very rarely got "clocked" by my voice in public. Not even a second look.

So what people say who knew you before is just how they have learned to associate your voice with "male" (understandably so).

I hardly ever, if ever, get pegged for my voice anymore. I cannot even remember the last time I was. But here is the key. Once I learned to love my voice and think to myself, "Ok, it sounds like a transgendered voice. So what? I am transgendered. I am still a woman. It still sounds like a female voice to most people. I have a great voice. I love my voice. Etc." You get the point. I decided to love my voice and accept it. Since that time, I have had no problems with being pegged for my voice. So learn to love your voice.

This goes back to people react to you the way you feel about yourself. If you are uncomfortable about some aspect of yourself, you will find people who will criticize you for that aspect. If you are comfortable with yourself, you will not. But do not be hard on yourself. We all are uncomfortable with things about ourselves. Over time, we become more and more comfortable and accepting and improve aspects of ourselves we do not like as well.

Changing your voice involves incorporating more female aspects to your voice as well as accepting parts of your old voice. You blend the old with the new. And a lot of the changes are very subtle.

As in walking and sitting (see the "Observation" section), listen to women talk. This is a great teacher. Then listen to men talk. Notice the differences. Men tend to lower their voices and talk more monotone. Women's voices are more sing song. They go up and down. They are much more expressive. This is probably one of those habits you un-learned to appear more masculine.

Thing Valley Girl. Think flamboyant. Think of ways you would have been made fun of for talking like in school. Not that you want to talk flamboyantly or like a Valley girl your whole life. But these are extreme feminine ways of talking. It will bring you out of your old way of talking and perhaps bring back ways you used to talk when you were younger and learned to suppress. Go extreme like these ways of talking and then pull back later. Do whatever helps you start to develop a more female way of talking.

Whispering or talking softer works at first as well. It will feminize your voice by taking off the harsh edges. Once again, you will not want to whisper the rest of your life, but it is great at first. It helps you get practice talking in a different way.

It is hard to do this at first for some people. It was for me. I was definitely what was called a "sissy" as a child. I talked very much like a girl. I got mistaken for my sister on the phone all the time. I was not trying to be this way. It was how I talked, and I got made fun of. As I said before, my own mother mocked the way I talked once and said I sounded like a "sissy. It caused me a lot of misery, so I learned to keep my mouth shut more and become more reserved. I learned to LOWER MY VOICE. I learned to talk monotone. I masculinized my voice! How ironic huh?

Now I never got to sounding exactly butch. But I lost the female tone to my voice over time in order to survive.

So, I had to unlearn these "masculine" habits I had developed with my voice. I had to try to get back to where I was as a child. This was tough after all those years of making myself try to sound like a man.

I instinctively lowered my voice now. I instinctively tried to not wave my arms and talk in a sing song manner because I was so criticized in the past.

All I really had to do was let go of those inhibitions and out came the female voice again.

So let go of some of your inhibitions. Be a little flamboyant if you want. Talk sing song. Talk like the women you know (if you like the way they talk, that is). Remember, this is a process. You will be modifying your voice over time. Who cares if it sounds extreme at first? You are breaking down old barriers and learning how to speak in a new way.

It is hard to let go of old engrained habits at first. Especially when you are living your life part time because you have to keep switching the way you talk. Do not fret. You will become a pro at switching back and forth. You are a TS. By your very nature you are very adaptable. We are chameleons in a way. It is one of our strengths.

Another thing you may be wondering about is how to switch voices if you are living part time. As I said, you will learn to switch at the drop of a hat. However, what about voicemail and answering the phone? How do you know which voice to use? I used an in-between voice and I just put my phone number on the voicemail instead of my name to stay somewhat "gender neutral". When I would answer the phone, I would just say "Hi" softly and then switch my voice appropriately for whoever was on the phone.

Here are some areas to work on, along with cautions that can actually make your voice sound fake when working on them. Once again, do not worry if your voice sounds fake at first. EVERYBODY has a fake sounding voice at first. It takes some practice.

1) Pitch – This is how high or low your voice is. The natural inclination is to make your voice high. We think that high = female. Not necessarily. Women's voices are actually not that much higher than men's (although they are higher usually). It is the singsong and demonstrative way they talk that makes it appear so much higher. In addition, there are women with low voices remember. You might want to sound like Minnie Mouse at first. This is not a natural sound! It is ok to do this at first though. You are retraining your voice. Just not the long term sound you want. So think, just a little. Less is more, as with everything. Raise it just a little bit. Then a little more after that if you're still not satisfied. But do not go too high or it will sound fake.

2) Vocabulary – Try to stop using crude or harsh words or swearing as much. Listen how women talk that you admire. Genetic women can get away with a bit more. People are watching you a bit more, so you cannot get away with quite as much swearing or crude talk usually.

3) Whispering – This is good and bad. Softening your voice will take the "male edge" off, especially at first. And this is good as a start. But you do not want to whisper your whole life. It does start to sound fakey. So what you want to do is soften your voice a bit, but do not whisper. Think "soft" and your voice will sound soft. It is very ok to whisper all you want at first though.

4) Singsong Quality – What this means is let your voice go up and down more. Do not talk monotone. Be expressive with your words. This is where Valley Girl comes in. It

kind of gives you an idea. So do Valley Girl, only pulled back. Go up at the end of your sentences more. Think of what you are saying and try to make your vocal tone express what you are saying, as well as your words.
5) Use your hands a bit more. I used to have to force my hands to stay still since my mother taught me this made me look feminine. Well, it does. Which is why that it is so great – a former weakness turned into a strength! And it is a way to be more expressive. Women use their hands to talk a lot, so if you want to, go for it.

Remember, just practice, practice, practice. Listen to women talk. Listen to yourself talk. Learn to love the old part of your voice as well as the new. This is what will make your voice sound natural – incorporating the old into the new. Soon you will have a feminine voice that you love and suits you.

Dating

Dating can be tricky in the TS world.

Do you like women? Men? Other TS's? A combination or all of the above?

Then there is the issue of what are you looking for. Just sex, casual dating, or something more serious. All of these are fine.

The problem is finding someone in your chosen attraction group that is also looking for someone like you and also is looking for the type of relationship (casual or serious) that you are.

Take heart that there are lots of people out there seeking out a special woman such as yourself. You just have to find them.

I would like to make a quick note here that it is important to realize and often misunderstood (especially by those outside the TG community) that gender identity and sexual orientation are two different things. Being a TS means you feel like a woman inside. Being gay means you are attracted to someone of the same gender. You can be a TS and still be attracted to women. Or you might be attracted to men. Or to both. It does not matter. That is your sexual orientation, not your gender. I think people do not understand why some TS women transition, but still want to be with a woman. Well, that is just who they are attracted to. But as a person, they identify inside as a woman. Of course, there are many TS women who are attracted to men or are bisexual, but I just wanted to clarify this distinction between gender and sexual orientation, as it can be confusing to some people.

The bulk of this section will deal more with people seeking more serious dating, but it is good for all to read, as you will eventually probably end up dating in one respect or another.

I realize that many of you may not want to date, or would like to strictly enjoy sex, without serious dating. That is perfectly fine! Whatever you want to do is just fine, as long as it is right for you. Some of what is in this section will still apply to those of you seeking something more casual. Be sure to read the "Safety" section as well.

Now, the first thing I would like to gently recommend is to not get into any serious dating at FIRST if you want to do more than just dress. You are going through enough without throwing that into the mix. TS's have the same dating problems everybody has – finding somebody compatible, breaking up with people you do not like, dealing with games people play, etc.

However, there is also the added problem that many people that like TS women want a specific kind of person. Preop, post-op, non-op, part time, full-time, totally passable, slutty looking, demure looking, etc. That is all fine (everybody has a right to want what they want), but what if what you are is not what they want, but they want to "make you" into that? TS women are hard to find, so if they find you, they might try to make you more into what they want.

Well you do not need somebody trying to force their agenda on you at this point. You are finding who you are. You do not want to end up being what somebody else wants. For example, they want a preop girl and you want to have SRS or be on hormones. What do you do? Or maybe they want postop and you do not want SRS. There are all kinds of things.

We all want love. I think as a TS we are sometimes even more anxious to find love and a loving partner. So it is easy for us to compromise who we are all over again to please a potential mate that we like.

That is what you have probably been doing your whole life though – compromising who you are to please other people (family, friends, society, etc). You have finally gotten the courage to take steps towards being who YOU want to be. Do not let anybody deter you from that.

YOU are your first priority. The dating will fall into place when it is meant to.

Oftentimes, these people that want a TS are experimenting. They are bi-curious or they saw a "shemale" porn movie and think that is how you will be (which may or may not be true) and want to try that. That is fine (and may fit what you are and are looking for), but you do not need to be anybody's experiment if you are seriously looking for a partner or are insecure about who you are at this point. You are at a fragile stage. Do not let yourself be used ever. You deserve more. Love yourself. Respect yourself and DEMAND the same in return! Once you do that, you will get love and respect back.

They may also be paranoid that somebody will find out. It is understandable, as they are just getting used to their attraction themselves and being different in their own way. However, do you want to come out of hiding and go through all this only to live in fear of being found out (for the reverse reason) for the rest of your life. No!

And everybody does have the right to want what they want. Nobody is bad for that. But you do not want somebody to make you do something YOU do not want. That is the key.

These are not evil or bad people. They are going through their own sort of transition, becoming comfortable with who they are. Also, someone is not bad for having their own preferences and wanting what they want. You just want to make sure what they want is what you want as well. Someone can be at the beginning stage of dating TS women when you meet them and still be a great dating prospect.

But the important thing if they are at this "beginning to date TS women" stage is that they are considerate of your feelings first. Also, trying to hide you is NEVER acceptable in my opinion. Why go out with somebody who is ashamed of you. Let them work that out for themselves first.

Now, for the record, my husband was at the experimentation stage when we met. So I did not follow my own advice, necessarily, but here is the key. He was considerate of my feelings and he always treated me like a lady. He was more worried about hurting me than about satisfying his fantasy. He was upfront about what he was looking for originally. We just happened to completely hit it off, and here we are 5 years later. It was a VERY bumpy five years, believe me, but still, it worked out. So you can still date a beginning guy. But make sure he is putting your feelings first. You are the one transitioning.

Once again, though, while you are developing your own sense of self and figuring out what you want, try to put dating to the side as much as possible. I know that is hard to do, and I did not even follow that advice myself. But if you can forgo serious dating at the beginning, do.

If you want to go to a club and flirt, that is fine and good, or to date casually. Gets you used to interacting with people as your female self. Just go there with the intent of just having fun and talking and dancing. I would not recommend going home with anybody you have just met, as there are TS haters out there and disturbed people. You do not want to put yourself at risk. Read the "Safety" chapter for more.

Now, after having said all that, I would also like to say that there are TONS of really nice men and women and TS women that are looking for a TS just like you out there. They are very respectful and very supportive and understanding and would just LOVE to find someone just like YOU! You just have to weed through the bad ones and find the one that is a good match for you (just like everybody has to do in dating). There are all types of people that like TS women as well, so whoever is your "type", there are people of that "type" looking for a TS women.

The right partner can be a tremendous source of support and friendship during your transition, if you can find one. Just remember to not compromise yourself or what you want. The best match is with a person who is looking for someone just like you and who is just the kind of person YOU are looking for. Not to say there will not ever be problems or things to work out (that is inevitable), but the basics are a good match.

Where can you go to meet people?

Online is one place and is both good and bad.

The internet is good because you have the safety of talking online first. Controlling when and where you meet more. Perhaps writing out in an online personal advertisement just what you are looking for and letting people come to you. The internet is a great place to find people looking for a TS as the rest of the world does not wear little signs on their foreheads (unfortunately) stating if they are open to or seeking a TS. Plus, as you become more and more passable and blend in, those who do like to date TS's will have trouble finding you since you are blending into society. So this is one good option to find these people.

The internet is bad as there are many people who are simply living out a fantasy and not really into reality. There are fake people. There are dangerous people. There are people who will not show up for a date. Regular people have these same problems with online dating, so it is not just a TS thing.

So when you want to meet someone, ensure you do it in a public place. Do not go over to their house. Do not have them over to your house. Once again, read the "Safety" section for more details on meeting people safely.

Now I am not trying to scare you. Most of the people will be nice. They will be interested and excited to meet you. They just might be scared, just like you. Realize that. And they might not show up. Just take it as par for the course.

Dating is very much like any other dating you might have done. It is a numbers game for one. You have to go on a lot of dates usually to find someone that is who you are looking for. And things may not work out. That is all part of dating, and a good thing. You date someone to find out if they are a good match. If someone is not interested in you or does not want to date you seriously, do not take it personally. It just means they are not the one for you. It really is not a rejection of you as a person or you as a TS. You are just fine. There is someone better out there for you. Just say, "Next!"

Have fun, though! Enjoy meeting new people. Enjoy being treated as your female self and interacting with people as the true you. It is truly a joyous experience when people first start treating you as the woman you are.

Another place you can meet people is at clubs or other social gatherings (perhaps a support group) where other TS's hang out. This can be great for meeting people in person. Just realize if you are looking for something serious that most of the people there are looking for sex, which is not in and of itself a bad thing.
However, I have known many girls who met their current partners at a club or social gathering.

Another way you might meet somebody is by them just walking up to you and asking you out in public (at the grocery store, at a restaurant, etc). They may recognize you are a TS, or they may not as you become very passable. You do not know if they know or not. What do you do?

Well, here is what to do.

Size them up a bit. Are they attractive to you? If yes, then keep talking. If not, just say I am dating someone or give them the cold shoulder or pretend you do not realize they are hitting on you. Playing dumb can be a great way to get somebody to back off without doing anything uncomfortable or hurting their feelings.

If they are attractive to you, how do you feel in your "gut" about them. Do they look "rednecky," rough, prejudiced? Of course, you could be totally wrong, but listen to your gut. Trust me, your initial gut reaction is usually right. If something makes you uncomfortable about them, once again, tell them you are dating someone, play dumb, etc. Better safe than sorry.

However, if you talk a bit and they seem like they would at least be nice if they found out, then you can chit chat with them. Meet them for a cup of coffee or a drink. Do not go somewhere private. They will usually give you an indication in that first meeting if they know (or just plain say something outright).

I am not sure you need to tell them until after a date or two if you feel they will not figure it out. If you are very passable and confident they will not know, you can wait to tell them. Why bother telling them if you go out on a date and do not hit it off.

Also, NO sex without telling them. That is unfair to them and also very dangerous for you. Do not ever put yourself in a potentially dangerous position like that.

Whenever you want to tell them (before the first date or after if you feel confident of your passability), you can then tell them. I would recommend telling them over the phone or even email at that point (you do not know them that well, so this is safest). This way, you are being fair to them and being respectful, but also protecting yourself before you start really liking them, in case they lose interest. Some will lose interest, some will not. But if you follow my advice, they will usually at least be polite. You are doing this respectfully and kindly and giving them an out. Remember, you did not ASK them to come up to you. They did it. So it is not your fault at this point.

As I said, some will stay interested. Some will not. It is all ok. This is dating! We all have people that like us or are not attracted to us. It does not mean we are undesirable or bad. And remember, you want to find someone who is looking for someone JUST like YOU. And who is just what you want! So it is ok if they fade away or say they are not interested. They will usually at least be polite as I said.

Now some who do stay interested (as more men are becoming interested in transgendered women than before), they might all of a sudden just be interested in sex. If that is all you want, then that is fine. If you want more, tell them so. You are in control of what you do, remember.

There is another interesting thing as you begin to date. It is a different dynamic for you now, if you dated before. Especially if you dated women only before or did not really date at all. If you are dating men, you may not realize how men act.

Before I go on, it is not my intent to make you think all men are pigs. There are tons of nice guys out there and I am not male bashing. However, if you are like I was when I started my transition (i.e. naïve), you may need to learn some things about how some men act.

Many men's main goal (with you as with genetic women) is to get you in bed. They can be very charming. They can act like they want more. If you just want sex, then that is ok. But if you want more, than watch them. They can be very manipulative of your feelings so that you will give in. Hold strong on the sex thing. If they want sex on the first one or two dates, it is a bad sign. I do not care what they say.

Men also are commitment phobic. Just realize this. Women have dealt with this for centuries. Hold out for what you want if you want more.

I am not bad mouthing sex. Sex is wonderful and an important part of a relationship. Just do not think you have to have sex to get a man to like you.

And there are many other things you will learn about handling men as you go along. They can be great, do not get me wrong. But if you are like me, I was naïve and innocent about men. I barely dated period before I transitioned, and I never acted or thought like a man, so I just did not know how men thought or acted.

When you transition, it is like you are a teenager again. Only this time, you are a teenage GIRL. And teenage girls have a lot to learn. Boys hurt them. Boys take advantage of them. They get too serious about a boy too quickly. They think they have to have sex to get a guy to stay with them or like them. I did ALL these things. Trust me, I was really dumb about dating and made lots of mistakes in my early transition. I did not have a Mom to tell me how guys act or what to do when I was dating. I was on my own.

However I really do not even look back at what I did as mistakes. I learned things. I became an empowered woman through it all. And the more empowered I became, the less heartache I got from dating. I also attracted a much better quality guy once I became empowered and respected myself.

Men will treat you the way you train them to treat you, as will people in general. Make sure you are treated as you like. And there are plenty of super nice, appreciate men and women out there who like TS's and would love to have a relationship with or date one. You are a rarity and a catch. Appreciate that!

As for any men or women reading this who want to date a TS woman, my intent is not to bad-mouth you. I know there are a lot of GOOD men (and women) out there who want to date a TS. Every TS is different, so it can be confusing as to how to treat them. My best advice on this is to just treat them with respect and as you would any women you went on a date with. Treat them like a woman. And do not be afraid to ask questions. How else will you know what they are looking for or what their preferences are? Every TS is different in what they want.

Just get to know them. And see if they are a good match for you as well. Just always be respectful and kind. TS's are dealing with a lot of issues as they transition, so they may be a bit more sensitive and you just need to be extra cautious in what you say sometimes and respectful of their feelings.

The bottom line is to be respectful, treat them like a woman, and do not be afraid to ask what they like and you will be ok. Treat them as you would any woman you are interested in, TS or not.

Safety

As both a woman and a transgendered person you are more vulnerable than you were living as a male. Living as a man, we sometimes do not realize or take for granted the very fact that we are male keeps a lot away from us. Criminals are less likely to mess with a man, thinking he is more likely to fight back, stronger than a woman and is less vulnerable than a woman. In addition, rapists typically target women, not men. Muggers are more likely to snatch a purse than steal a wallet out of your pocket. There is also the added issue of bigots out there filled with hatred. They may want to hurt you simply because you are transgendered.

Now, the point of this section is not to scare you. Nor should you go around in fear or fear this will happen to you. In fact, if you dwell on fear or think some homophobe or neo-Nazi or criminal is going to attack you, you might just attract that into your existence. Do not live in fear. You are a brave person for doing this. Most people will not even notice you or, if they do, not care. Even if someone does not like you, they will more than likely give you about 2 seconds thought and then be on their way. So this is not a caution to live in constant fear.

However, you do need to behave differently and be more aware of your surroundings now that you are a woman and a TS. I was rather naïve about these things, and break out in a cold sweat thinking of some dumb things I did or precautions I did not take. But I have learned a lot, and I will share these with you now.

Most of these are common sense and most of these relate simply to how women must behave a little differently then men by virtue of them being women.

So here is a list of safety tips and precautions:

1) Hold your purse securely over your shoulder.

The first thing is simply learn to hold your purse right to avoid it being snatched. You want to wrap the strap around your shoulder and carry it under your arm and hold on to the strap. That will pretty much do it. Or if the purse has a really long strap, I have even seen women wrap it around one side of their neck and then have it hang on the opposite side of their body. That will hold it to you.

2) Learn to be aware of your surroundings.

Do not be paranoid. Do not be seeking rapists, murderers and thugs at every turn. Not like that. Just simply be aware as you are walking to your car for example. I tend to daydream a lot. This is usually ok if you are in a crowded public place. But if you are walking alone through a parking lot or down a street, it is safest to be alert and do not daydream so much then.

3) Walk like you are sure of yourself and know where you are going.
This projects strength, not vulnerability. This alone will keep away a lot of the bad guys. Focus on where you are going and walk confidently. If you do not feel sure of yourself, fake it. Interestingly enough, if you start walking LIKE you have confidence, pretty soon you will start FEELING confident inside. Mind-body connection.

4) When meeting someone, make sure you meet them in a public place.

Meet for a cup of coffee or dinner. If they will not do that because they are scared somebody will know, that is their loss. Not yours. There are plenty of men and women out there. You do not need to compromise your safety. They are more than likely perfectly safe, but you just never know, so you have to be safe. Do not invite them to your house until you have met them several times and really know them and feel comfortable with them. Do not go to THEIR house until you have met them several times and feel comfortable with them. Make sure a friend knows their name and phone number. Remember, women get raped by men they do not know. And you do not know what his hang-ups or agenda are. Once again, most of the men and women are fine so do not become paranoid. You just have to be smart and play it safe.

5) Always follow your gut.

If you feel uncomfortable or nervous in a situation, get out. We all have a sixth sense that is there to protect us. Who cares what people think. If a person makes you uncomfortable and makes you want to get away from some reason and you are not sure why, just excuse yourself to go to the Ladies room or say you see a friend across the room. Or if you are out alone and feel that, get to your car or in a public place as quickly as you can.

6) When walking to your care, have your keys ready.

That way you can get right in the car and will not be fumbling with your keys. This is when muggers or carjackers or rapists usually get someone. The victim is distracted trying to get into their car.

7) If you go out to a club or a place like that, go with a friend.

There is safety in numbers. People will usually leave you alone if you are with somebody.

8) If you are leaving someplace and a guy is following you or something, go back in and get someone to walk you to your car.

Get a security guard or bouncer or the manager or a friend to walk out with you. I have had a few strange incidents with this and will relate one of the funniest and one to learn from.

I had a guy chase me around a mall once. No lie. The guy saw me in a grocery store first and aggressively tried to get a date. I said no and moved on and did not give it any more thought. Then I went to the grocery store a couple days later. There he was and this time he followed me out to my car and grabbed my arm and said he wanted to take a walk with me in the mall. And I just stopped, looked him in the face, and said no. NO way was I moving further until he let go. Then like a month or two later, I am walking through the mall near the store, and who do I run into but Mr. Grocery store lothario. So I see him and turn the other way. He starts following me. I walk faster. He walks faster. I cut into Barnes and Noble, and he follows me. So I'm running around the store trying to lose him. It was kind of comical looking back if it had not creeped me out. So I got out of the store and walked as quickly as I could through the mall, out and to my car. Fortunately I was taller than him so I lost him. In all honesty, I think he was harmless, and I was more mad then scared, but still. Looking back, I probably should have reported him to security after the third time. Better safe than sorry. Do not worry how you look or that you are being paranoid. If somebody is making you uncomfortable, be safe.

9) Do not worry about hurting someone's feelings or causing a scene if you feel threatened.

As human beings in a polite society and as women in general, we tend to not want to hurt people's feelings or cause a scene. What if he is harmless? What if I look like a fool? Women get attacked for this reason. They are afraid to scream out or make a scene. It is crazy, but true. So if you feel threatened or harassed by somebody or are being attacked even, scream bloody murder, run to a security guard, whatever. CAUSE A SCENE. That alone will make the guy run.

10) If you are being attacked, do not worry about being a lady.

In other words, do not be afraid to fight back and let your testosterone kick in and fight back. This does not mean you are a man. But you have a strength in your male side, in the testosterone you have that can give you an advantage in a fight. Use it if you have to. We are talking about your safety and maybe your life.

Coming Out

Telling friends, family, and work about yourself is a very personal decision, and a very difficult one. In many ways, I think it is the hardest part of the transition. None of us want to be rejected. And nobody particularly likes change, and we are worried that everything WILL change after we tell people, which it does, but not necessarily for the worst. In fact, it will change for the better because we will be more free to be ourselves.

Still, we worry about losing people – friends, family. Of hurting people. We have guilt for doing this.

Fear of telling people is what holds many of us back for years from doing anything.

Remember, though, we cannot always make everybody else happy. This does not mean we do not want to be kind or care about people. But everybody has to at some point in their life do something that will hurt somebody else, even though that is not their goal. For example, pursue a career different than their parents wanted or ask for a divorce from an unhappy marriage. Etc.

On the other hand, I think telling people is also one of the most personally rewarding and freeing things we can do.

Now you may just want to tell a close friend or family member or your spouse. You may not be at the stage or even want to go full time – which is the only time you really have to tell the whole world. In either case, you still have to figure out the right way to do it, even if you are just telling one person.

If you are at this point, you usually feel you do not have any choice. You just feel you HAVE to do this or you will go crazy or something. You are ready to be you. You feel like you are going to burst. Staying in hiding is more psychologically hurtful then making a change. This is a powerful place to be as it will ease or even erase the fear.

I know for years, I was HORRIFIED of telling people. I could not imagine having the courage to tell people. To do this. To be so different! To stand out. To risk losing people. To risk being made fun of. To risk changing things "as is". "As is" may have been miserable, but at least I knew what it was.

However, when the time came to tell people, that fear just disappeared. I had some apprehension, yes. But I just was so sure of myself and that this was me, that the fear went away. I wanted to be me. I really felt like I had no choice, but that was an empowering feeling, not a disempowering feeling.

Give yourself the chance to feel that way. You will just know when it is time to "come out." Nobody can tell you when. Only you can. Trust your inner voice. Listen to it. If you don't feel it's the right time, don't do it. You will just KNOW when it is.

Work with your therapist on this. They can certainly give you some support and guidance.

People tell in different ways. Some just blurt it out (not the best way, but at least it gets it over with). Some tell it in person in a planned situation. Some write a letter. Some tell on the phone so they do not have to see the other person's face. Some send an email.

I used all of these methods, depending on who I was telling (although I do not think I ever blurted it out).

However, I am a BIG believer in the letter. This is how I told most people (except work, which I will get to later). However, you may use different ways for different people, depending on the situation.

The letter has several advantages:

1) You can work out your thoughts on paper and say it how you want to. When you are talking to someone in person or on the phone, emotions will take over and you might forget things or get caught up in a fight or answering questions or defending yourself or something like that. You cannot control how you tell them or what you say as much.
2) You can tell as much or as little as you want to.
3) You do not have to see people's faces when they hear, which can be traumatic. The letter shields you from their initial reactions.
4) People who read it can have time to have whatever reaction they want without worrying about hurting you. They can sit there and study it and think about it. They can feel mad or amazed or whatever and not worry about hurting your feelings as they are entitled to their initial feelings too.

Now, if you would still like to tell someone in person, that is ok. Do what you feel comfortable with. What you feel is right. But I would still write a letter first to get your thoughts organized and down.

My letter to my family and some close friends ended up being about 7 or 8 pages. I think I probably should have put chapters in looking back! It does not need to be that long, unless you want. It can be as long or as short as you want. But for me, I wanted to explain some of my history. When I started feeling this (as a child). Experiences I had. Explain I did not want to hurt them. I wanted to explain what a TS was. There was a lot to cover. So I put that all in there. Of course, I did not tell work or acquaintances this much.

Think about it. What would you like to tell whoever you are coming out to? What would you like to share? Put your heart into it, and you cannot go wrong. Write it all out. Modify it. Play with your letter. Read it to your therapist or a friend who already knows.

Some things you might want to cover in your letter (pick and choose what you want to talk about):

1) What is a ts (or a cd, tv, drag queen, whatever it is you want to tell them about) – they may have no idea. Many people I know did not.
2) When you started feeling this way
3) Some things you went through as a child or prior to this in regards to being transgendered.
4) Reassure them about their feelings and that they are ok.
5) Steps you are taking in your transition.
6) Signs they may have seen that you were like this. For example, were you feminine as a child? Did you put on makeup ever? Etc.

Who should you tell first? Well it is good if you have a friend you can really trust and who you think would be open to tell that person first. It might be a sibling. It all depends too on how far you plan on going. Only if you plan on living full time as a female, do you need to tell work, friends (unless you want them to know), etc. Usually just immediate family is necessary. Even then it may not be. Only you know your situation and how you want to live and how far you want to go. But I would tell immediate family first. Then friends (if going full time or you want them to know). Then work (if going full time).

How to tell work is something we all worry about. Check any human resources manuals you have access to. What is your "gut feeling" about your company. Do they seem open? Are you in constant contact with the public, or more to yourself or strictly in the office. In the latter case, they will probably care less as there is no risk of you affecting clientele, which you probably would not anyway.

If you REALLY feel that your company might fire you or make your life miserable after you go full time (due to a rough work atmosphere or unaccepting coworkers), then you might want to search for another job or start your own business.

Do not assume though that you will be fired. I believe that companies are becoming more open than they used to be. Many companies see it as a feather in their cap to be non-discriminatory and open. Your company may be like that. Just follow your gut on this.

Plus, a good employee is a good employee. It is expensive to train a new person. Be the best employee you can be. Go out of your way more than usual. Make friends with as many coworkers as you can. Be likeable and easy-going. Become as valuable as you can to them. They really will not want to lose you.

This is what I did. I also without realizing I did it, became liked by the President of the company. It was a smaller company (50 people – easier to make an impact in a smaller place, by the way). So when the news came out, this President was supportive of me. Some people were uncomfortable, some not. The second in command apparently said fire me. But most people were supportive. And because I had that President on my side, I was ok. Not to mention many managers and coworkers who supported me. People liked me. They became my best defense when things were going on I did not know about.

So, make friends. Be likeable. Be easy going. Be invaluable. You will have an army of people sticking up for you when you do not even realize it. And as I have said, they will not want to lose you if you are a good, valuable employee. You being a TS in most cases will NOT affect your job unless you are perhaps in sales dealing with a lot of ultra-conservative or "rednecky" clients. For the most part, people just want to know you can do your job and make them money or satisfy their needs.

You will want to go to your Human Resources person first. I would recommend doing this in person, although you can do it by letter. Answer any questions they have. Talk about when you would like to go full time. Work out a plan for how to tell everybody and when you will do this. Offer to be open to answer questions people might have (as long as they are respectful). Work with them on how to handle the bathroom situation.

For the bathroom situation, I would recommend at first using the ladies restroom in the lobby if you are in a big building rather than the one on your floor. You can do this for a couple of months (or another agreed upon time) and then start using the one on your floor. Or you might have a bathroom buddy that will go with you and watch out when you go in there. People work out all kinds of procedures. It is all very doable.

Some women may be uncomfortable at first with you using the Ladies room, but after they work with you a couple of months in your new female role, they will become more comfortable (at least most of them) and it will not be an issue.

Your Human Resources department and you can then work out how to tell everybody.

In my case, they told all the managers in the Monday morning meeting. I told my boss and the two guys I worked with (I was in IT). Then the managers each told their people in separate meetings all on the same day. It was an interesting feeling walking in that morning. I knew everything would change that day as everybody was about to find out.

People were pretty supportive for the most part in my coming out. Some people were ok at first, and then kind of kept their distance from me. Some people I thought would really have a problem were very supportive.

Do not prejudge anybody. You just do not know how people will react (coworkers, friends, family). Some will react badly that you thought would be ok. Some will react GREAT that you thought would react badly. You just do not know.

However, if you are ok with yourself and tell people compassionately and answer their questions, most people will pleasantly surprise you. And more and more people know about TS's than they used to due to more documentaries on television about transgendered people, so that makes it somewhat easier.

Even if people do not react well, you have done what you should do. You behaved with dignity and class and compassion and honesty. That is all you can do. You cannot control how people feel, nor is that your job.

As you tell people, allow them to have whatever reaction they want. It does not affect who you are. Kind of separate yourself from that. If someone is abusive, you have the right to tell them to stop or walk out of the room. People have a right to their reactions, but you have the right to protect yourself.

People have a variety of reactions. I experienced all of these from people I told:

1) Support – Many people will be very supportive of you, even if it takes them some time to get used to it.

2) Confusion – They might not understand exactly what a transsexual is.
3) Concern – They may be worried you are confused or doing something that will hurt you.
4) Shock – They had no idea
5) Anger – You are disrupting their life and taking away their image of you
6) Hurt – You are taking away their image of you. To some people, they are losing the old you. It is almost like the "old you" has died, and they miss that person. Yes you are the same person, but nevertheless, they are losing that old image of you.
7) Judgment – Some may think you are selfish or sinning against God, etc
8) Discomfort – They may not know how to act around you at first.

Also, realize, that people's initial reactions are just that – initial. There may have some of the negative reactions above, but then they will be fine later. For example, one of my sisters (who is very conservative and religious) was rather mean to me and not supportive at all at first. We did not talk for a couple of years. Today, she is SO nice to me. She treats me just like her sister and is very supportive of me. You just never know. I also had a couple of friends that made it a point to say they supported me and then started to avoid me and the friendships just kind of faded away. That is ok too. They have that right.

You want positive, supportive people in your life. Take this attitude. The people that "fade away" or are not supportive will naturally be eliminated from your life and supportive people will come in to take their place. Everything will work out for the best.

Remember, most people will end up supporting you. And if they do not, they will usually move out of your life and somebody supportive will move in. Besides which, at this point, you are moving towards your dream and being you and that is so liberating that you can handle someone not being there for you anymore.

This is a scary process, oftentimes, I realize. But if you want to live full time or be yourself, it is necessary. More than anything though, it is one of the most liberating things you will ever do FOR YOURSELF. You deserve this. The burden of staying in hiding will be lifted. You can be you now. Trust me, that is one of the best things you will ever do for your mental health.

I still remember taking the letter to my siblings to the mailbox. They were the first people I was going to tell. I stood by that mailbox for 5 minutes I bet, putting the letters in, then pulling them back. Knowing I could not take it back once I dropped the letters in the box. Then finally, I just said, "Enough," and I dropped the letters in the mailbox, and I knew my life would never be the same.

And you know what, after a moment of a knot in my stomach, I was not scared anymore. I felt free. Empowered. I practically skipped back home! At that point, it was done and out of my hands.

And the rest followed.

It will seem like you are constantly telling people for awhile. Not only your friends and family and coworkers. Your mailman. Your neighbors (although I didn't even bother, I let them just wonder). Etc.

If you are going full time, everybody needs to know. But after awhile, you won't blink an eye. Once you have told a few, there is nothing you cannot do. It truly is empowering.

I would also like to tell you about a little trick you can use to gently start giving people an idea before you go full time (if this is applicable). It kind of keeps things from being a total shock. You can subtly start giving people an idea something is up without actually telling them.

As you transition, there are some things you can do on the outside to start feminizing yourself without completely feminizing yourself. What you want to do is be a little more androgynous. Wear a woman's mock turtleneck maybe if you have the guts for that. Or wear a woman's watch. Pluck or wax your eyebrows (this will make you appear more feminine). Wax your arms. Grow out your hair more. Even getting facial hair removed will give people some idea. However, they more than likely will not have the guts to say anything (or will feel it would be rude to say something). Simple little things like that will give people a little sign. Then when you do tell them, they will think, I thought something was up.

You do not have to do any of these "soft hints". Just do one or two if you are comfortable with them. It is a great exercise in learning to be yourself as well and be a little different. It starts to build up your courage more and more as you learn to do something "out of the ordinary".

There is also the issue of what pronoun you would like people to call you (i.e. "he" or "she"). You will need to tell people how to refer to you so they know. Different TS have different wishes on how they wish to be referred to. Some want to be referred to as "she" all the time, even if they are part time. Others wish to be referred to as "she" only when they appear as their female self. The same issue holds true with your "male" and "female" names.

To me, when you are part time, it is easiest if people refer to you as whatever gender you are appearing on the outside. For example, at work, people would still call you "he" and by your male name. If you meet a friend as your female self, then they would refer to you as "she" and your female name. If you do not like this and want to always be called one pronoun or the other, then that is just fine, too. Just let people know.

If you go full time, of course, you will want to always be referred to as "she" and by your female name. People will make mistakes with this for awhile, mainly because they are breaking an old habit. They are used to calling you by a certain gender pronoun and by your old name.

They usually do not mean this offensively at all. It is strictly a habit. They have known you by your old name and gender for years, so they just have to get out of this habit. Do not fret too much about this at first. They will slip less and less the longer you live full time as a woman. Soon the old you will fade more from their mind and they will relate to you more as your new "true" self.

People who have only known you as your female self will not have this same problem, unless they are just ignorant, in which case you can correct them.

As you go through this coming out process (even if it is only to tell a trusted friend), you will feel so liberated. The fear of being "found out" will be lifted. You can truly start to be you, and that is a wonderful feeling!

Dealing with Criticism and Judgments from Others

"He who trims himself to suit everyone will soon whittle himself away." ~Raymond Hull

Most of us want to be liked by others. We do not want to hurt those we love. We do not like to be criticized or judged.

I realize there are some people out there who are completely self-confident and unaffected by others, but this is not usually the case with transsexuals (and most people, in fact). It is one reason we wait so long to start our transition – because of fear of criticism, hurting others, etc.

Criticism and judgment usually happen when we are first telling people. One thing to keep in mind (as I mentioned in the "Coming out" Chapter) – people's initial reactions will not necessarily match their ultimate reactions. So just let them react how they react at first. Some people react negatively at first, and then come to be very accepting.

Remember in all of this, you do not ever have to accept abuse. You have the right to say, stop that. And if they do not, you have the right to walk out of the room, get out of that situation, etc.

Here are some fears we deal with:

1) Fear of hurting our families and those we love.
2) Fear of criticism and judgment.
3) Fear of not being liked
4) Fear of losing people
5) Fear of standing out
6) Fear of not being accepted

Realize that fear is like planning something bad happening. The thing is, these bad things usually do not happen, so take heart. Try to picture something good happening instead.

Here are some helpful hints to deal with these fears. I will respond to each of these fears separately.

1) Fear of Hurting Those we Love

This is a legitimate fear. We love these people. We do not want to hurt them. Unfortunately, in life, we cannot always spare everyone's feelings. This is part of the journey of life. To be ourselves, we do hurt people sometimes, although that is not our purpose or intention. You are not setting out to hurt these people. You just ARE who you are. They all get to live their lives, and you have probably been accepting of them. Why should they not be accepting back? What you do really has no affect on their life (unless it is a spouse or children). You are not doing anything to hurt them. If they feel hurt, it has more to do with their own, quite frankly, selfish (unless they are a spouse or child) concerns. We all have to take a stand at some point in our lives to be who we are and do what WE want. Otherwise, you are not living your life fully. Remember, you are the only one who has to live your life. They do not. You are not being unfeeling or unloving. You are just respecting and loving yourself.

2) Fear of criticism

Most of us do not like to be criticized or judged. Just realize, when people criticize you, it has more to do with THEM than you. This is their own internal criticism coming out against you. You are making THEM uncomfortable, which is their problem, not yours. You just cannot make everybody happy and comfortable. The audience is fickle. So stop worrying about what everybody thinks. But be gentle with yourself. This is a hurdle that takes a little time to get over, and that is ok. As you transition, you will become more and more confident and independent. Sometimes if criticism bothers us, it indicates something we are criticizing ourselves for as well. Be gentle on yourself. Love yourself. Talk these things over with a friend or your therapist who understands. You are not a bad person for being who you are. That is what you are on this planet to be – YOURSELF!

3) Fear of not being liked

This goes along with number 2 really. You cannot be liked by everybody. Nobody on this planet is liked by everybody. You probably were not liked by everybody before your transition either. Just think to yourself, oh well. If they do not like you, they have that right. You have the right to not hang around with them and to tell them to go bug off if they are bothering you. Once again, as you progress in your transition, you will begin to feel more and more empowered and like YOURSELF more and more, so it will not bother you as much if somebody does not like you.

4) Fear of Losing People

This can be a paralyzing fear. We do not want to lose someone we love or are friends with. It is a risk of transitioning. When I started out, this was one of my biggest fears (along with hurting people). However, at the same time, I thought, I am resenting these people for holding me back. Yet I was not giving them a chance to accept me. In my experience, this fear, like all fears, is mainly in our head. You have to give people the chance. Most people will be accepting, eventually at least. If they abandon you, well then, they were not truly a friend. You want people that love you for you and accept you for you. This is one of those painful parts of the transition, but you come out after this process of losing some people so much healthier mentally. You are surrounded by those who truly love you for you and accept you for you.

5) Fear of standing out and being different

The fact is, most of us do want to fit in and be like everybody else. It is easier. We can kind of glide through life. We fit into "the pack". However, as a TS, you will be different. You are kind of a "misfit" amongst your family and friends as you are a third gender, different from all of them. You might walk in a room and get a look.

This fear is easily overcome though. I have learned a couple of tricks.

First off, think to yourself, it is good to be different. Anybody can be like anybody else. I am different and special. Keep saying this to yourself: "It is good to be different". Once you get this in your head, standing out will not bother you too much.

Second, when you enter a room, if you are nervous about what people will think, think to yourself, "All you people like me". If you are going into a club and want to meet a guy, think "You guys want me". People respond to that somehow. It gives you a confident air. They will like you.

Third, realize that as you transition, you will not stand out as much as you become more and more passable. Also, as you transition, you will become more and more confident and stop worrying about standing out.

6) Fear of not being accepted

As with the previous fears, you will worry about this less and less as you transition and become accepting of yourself. And once you accept yourself, just as you are, and think you are just fine, other people will as well. If you accept yourself, so will other people. Also, if somebody does not accept you, you do not need them in your life. That is their issue. Big deal. There are plenty of other people out there who do accept you!

Finally, one general tip for dealing with insecurity and fearful feelings. Learn to "switch off" your thinking when it gets negative. Think of your brain like a switch. For example, you catch yourself worrying that the lady at the next table just gave you a disgusted look after "clocking" you. Turn it off. Think of something else. Scared of walking into a room? Find yourself picturing a negative response? Turn it off. Either think of nothing or think of something else. Better yet, think of something positive. Think, "That lady is giving an ugly face to the waiter not seeing her motion for service." Think, "these people are gonna love me. Everybody loves me!"

Another thing, learn to get out of yourself. Stop worrying what everybody is thinking of you. Start thinking of what you are doing, what you want for dinner, where you are walking to, what is the price on that dress in the store, etc. In other words, live your life and stop worrying about everybody else. They are too busy with their own business for the most part to worry about you. People are not going to be watching you unless you THINK they are.

Your New Name

Here is another fun part of transitioning. You get to pick a new name! The name YOU want. Not the name somebody else (namely, your parents) picked for you. How many of us get stuck with names we do not like.

This can just be a name you use when you go out as a female or are expressing your female side. Or this may be your permanent name if you choose to live full time as a female (in which case you will need to change your name, of course).

So, what is a name you have always liked? Say that with your last name. How do they sound together? How about a middle name? How does that flow with your first and last name. You can even change your last name if you want.

Now, as I said, if you have no desire to live full time as female, this is just your "female" name you will use when going out as your female self or talking to people as your "female" self. However, if you do want to live full time as a female, you are going to want to legally change your name.

If the latter (i.e. you want to permanently change your name), give this some thought. Play around with a lot of different names. Also, remember you will be living with this name now. You will be telling everybody this name. So Destiny Larue may sound great for a part time name or Amber Luvsalot, but do you want to have to tell your boss that is your name? You get my point.

But still, have fun. Find a name you feel fits you and your personality. A name you like the sound of. A name that fits with your last name (old or new if you want to change the last name). I played around with names for a few months before settling on mine and it just "felt" right. It fit me somehow and it fit with my last name to boot.

Now, for changing your name legally. This is not that big of a deal. People change their names all the time. Divorced women want to revert back to their maiden name, for example. Or somebody just wants a new first name. It is done all the time.

The process will vary from state to state, and county to county, but here are the basic steps you will want to do.

The name change is done at the county level. So contact your local County Clerk's office and say you would like to legally change your name. They will be able to tell you what you need to do. More than likely they will even have a written out procedure they can give you to follow.

You do not need to have a lawyer for this. You can just do this yourself.

There will be some basic paperwork to fill out. You will need to pick a court date for the hearing to change your name (do not be intimidated, it is very routine and quick). I would recommend picking a date after you go full time.

You will probably have to place an advertisement in a local paper in the Legal Notices section stating that you are changing your name. The County Clerk will probably give you the wording for this advertisement. This is done in order to prevent people from changing their names to avoid creditors and such. You usually have to do this several weeks before the court date and have it published a certain number of weeks in a row.

Then on your court date you will go to the courthouse. They will tell you where to go.

This is how mine went. Yours may be a bit different, but probably will be similar.

You will be in a courtroom with a bunch of other cases. It is kind of like small claims or traffic court almost.

Your case will be called. You will go up. The Judge will look at the paperwork. Ask a couple simple questions like are you trying to defraud or get out of bills by changing your name. You will say no. He will sign the paperwork.

Voila, your name is changed!

You will then need to get some certified copies and start changing your name on various documents. Your driver's license and your Social Security card first off. For these you will need to go in in person to change. It is not a big deal. They deal with hundreds of people every day and have dealt with plenty of name changes. They will not blink an eye. They will just need to see the name change order. You will need to get your new Social Security card probably prior to changing your name legally at work for your checks.

You will also want to change the name on all your bills, at work (for your checks), your bank accounts, your mortgage and title and any other legal documents that have your name on them.

Do not worry about forgetting to change something. You will eventually get a piece of paper or a bill with your old name on it and that will remind you. As long as you have a copy of your name change order, you are always covered.

Most of your bills will just require you to fax or mail a copy of the name change certificate. Some may have a form to fill out. It is all pretty simply. Credit cards and mortgages may require a certified copy of the name change order.

As far as your birth certificate, you do not necessarily need to change this unless you need to show your birth certificate a lot, which most of us do not. However, if you do or you just want to change it, then you just need to contact the state where you were born. They will tell you what you need to do to get your name changed on the birth certificate.

They will not change your gender unless you have had SRS, and each state is different on the requirements. Some states will never change it. However, you do not really need to worry about that too much at this time.

But while you are finding out how to change your name on your birth certificate, you can ask them about their rules for changing your gender as well. Do not be self conscious about asking these questions. Public agencies deal with thousands of people. They do not have time to worry too much about what you are doing. It is just business. And besides which, in those thousands they deal with all the time, a few are going to be TS's, so it is probably not going to even be news to them. I would recommend changing your gender and name on your birth certificate at the same time.

Helpful Insights 4

1) **Do not focus on any single part of your body too much.**

In other words, look at your overall image. For example, I have met beautiful TS women who hate their feet or their hands and think they are too big. They have gone through their whole transition and they let that one part of their body they dislike make them miserable.

We all have some part of our body that is less than we would like probably. Do not focus on that. Focus on your overall appearance, your health, your happiness, etc. Pretty soon you will stop worrying about that part you hate and perhaps even come to appreciate and love it as you should!

2) **Love every part of your body.**

It is not healthy to hate any part of your body, and that includes your penis (no offense is meant by this term, it is strictly used for reference purposes here. I realize many TS prefer to call it a clitoris, as I do). You may not want your penis. That is ok. But do not HATE it. It is part of you. Over time, you may even begin to appreciate the beauty and femininity of it (believe it or not). You do not have to use it as a man would sexually. Embrace it as part of your uniqueness. Love yourself. That includes loving every part of your body and seeing it as perfect. You can still have SRS. But do not HATE your penis (or your big feet or nose, or whatever it is you hate about your body).

3) **"Things" do not make you a woman.**

You just ARE a woman. SRS, hormones, makeup, hair, etc do not make you a woman. They help you appear more as a woman on the outside, but they do not MAKE you a woman.

It is easy to get caught up in feeling that these things do make us a woman. For a long time, I associated my hair with making me look female. Now I do not. Or at the very beginning, I used to HAVE to wear makeup if anybody saw me as I felt that transformed me. And that is ok. At the beginning we need these things such as makeup and clothes to help us feel like we are appearing as our female selves and to give us confidence. But over time, you will not need these things to make you feel you are a woman. You will realize you already ARE. A drug or operation will not do that either. Once you stop relying on outside 'things" to make you a woman or make you feel like a woman, you will have a sense of peace and happiness you did not have before.

These outside things are not bad. In fact, they are wonderful, and you can still appreciate them. Just do not feel you need them to make you a woman.

Facial Feminization Surgery (FFS)

Before I get into this section, I want to caution you to not become a plastic surgeon addict. Many girls do (TS and genetic). Your face is part of who you are. It has its own beauty. You do not, in my opinion, want to do so much facial surgery you come out looking like a plastic Barbie or every other TS out there who has had full facial feminization surgery.

Remember, your face is part of what makes you "you". It is something unique to you. You do not want to necessarily totally change it and not be able to recognize yourself afterwards. This is more about enhancing your own unique look and beauty, rather than completely changing it.

I have seen girls get facial surgery that, quite frankly, looked just fine and very feminine beforehand. They really did not need it. But they become convinced they should. Sometimes they came out looking less natural and worse than before.

Facial feminization is not a requirement, nor do you always need it to be passable. So do not go overboard here or you might end up looking fake or worse than you do now. Do not start picking apart every little part of your face because it does not look like the "ideal woman". You will never be satisfied if you get in this habit. Learn to appreciate your unique beauty.

That being said, facial feminization can be very beneficial in some cases. What do I mean by facial feminization?

There are certain subtle differences (some not so subtle) between men's and women's faces. For example, women have higher eyebrows. Women have a smooth forehead. Men usually have to one degree or another a certain projecting "brow" – if you look at a man's profile, there will be some jutting bone above the eyebrows. Men have an Adam's apple. Women do not. Women will have fuller cheekbones usually. You get the picture.

The bottom line with plastic surgery is if something really bothers you, and you want to change it and can afford it, then that is just fine. However, make sure it is really bothering YOU and not somebody else. In other words, do not feel you need to do full facial feminization surgery simply because many in the TS community say you need to do it to look totally feminine. Do not expect facial surgery to make you happy with yourself. You have to be happy with yourself already.

However, the right facial surgery can do wonderful things.

I would recommend the following surgeries only:

1) Tracheal Shave – In this surgery, the tissue in the front of your Adam's apple is shaved so that you no longer have an Adam's apple. If you do have an Adam's apple, you will want to do this surgery eventually as people look for an Adam's apple when trying to see if you are a TS. Why give them anything to look at? Not everybody has a noticeable Adam's apple, so you may not need to do this.
2) Frontal Bossing (I call it a Brow Shave) – This involves removing protruding bone above the eyebrows and perhaps raising the eyebrows to give a more feminine appearance. I would only do this if you have a very pronounced brow or really feel the need to lift your eyebrows. However, you can often do a lot of lifting your eyebrows with the proper waxing or plucking.
3) Breast Augmentation – If you cannot or do not want to do hormones or just do not have much breast growth from hormones, this can give you the breasts you want. Do not go too big. Be proportional. A full B or C cup is fine for most women. Follow the surgeon's recommendation. Keep in mind, your cup size will usually increase a half to

a full cup size after about a year due to the implants settling, so just keep this in mind when picking a cup size. I went from a C to a D cup myself in a year.

There are some other surgeries you might consider. Just be careful. A lot of these can be overdone and are not needed often. So do not let a surgeon talk you into doing them if you are satisfied with your face. Just change what is bothering you. These surgeries are not in and of themselves bad. They are just not needed many times.

1) Cheekbone implants – Women typically have fuller cheekbones. Be careful with this. Too full cheekbones can look fake or make you look unpassable almost. Too big and people call them "drag queen cheekbones" (no offense intended to anybody). So only do this if you have NO cheekbones and only have small implants put in.
2) Rhinoplasty (nose job) – If your nose really bothers you or is too big, a good nose job can make you look more feminine. Just be careful here too. I used to think my nose was a bit big, but then I got so I liked it. It really is in proportion to my face and it is part of what makes me unique. Nose jobs can turn out bad sometimes too. So only do this if you really hate your nose. If you do really hate it and can afford it, then by all means do it.
3) Scalp and Hairline Lowering – Here they can bring your hairline down lower. Women typically have lower hairlines, although there are women with very high foreheads out there.
4) Lip Augmentation – This will give you fuller lips. BE CAREFUL. Too full lips look fake and not very attractive. Genetic women can overdo this too. I would only recommend this if your lips are very thin or you only augment them a VERY small amount.
5) Chin reduction or augmentation – This is to make your chin in proportion to the rest of your face. It can give your

face a more rounded look. If you choose to do this, it is convenient to do it at the same time as the tracheal shave, as these are both in the same area.

These are the main surgeries out there. There are several plastic surgeons out there who can work with you on this. Talk with your therapist about this. Remember, do not overdo. Do a little at a time.

I would not recommend full facial surgery at once. Do what bothers you most. You may not want the rest done later. What you have done may be enough.
I was going to go the full facial feminization route thinking I had to, and only ended up doing a Tracheal Shave with a little bit of chin reduction, along with breast augmentation. I am very happy with my face. I am glad I did not do more. My face is part of me and it is very feminine already. So I am glad I took my time and thought about it and did not go in for the whole surgery at once.

Another reason to not do everything at once is that facial feminization surgery hurts. Especially if they are working on the bone. And you will have swelling and recovery time. Do a little at a time to make recovery easier.

A final reason to not do too much too soon. There is an interesting thing that happens with our view of our face. When we first start out, we see our face as masculine. We have been trained to see our face as a man's face because that is how we have had to live.

However, as we go full time and are living as a woman, we stop seeing our face as a man's face, and more and more as a woman's face. We do learn to see its femininity and beauty.

That is why I caution you to not hurry into a bunch of facial surgery at once. Give yourself time to see your face as a woman's. Give yourself time to think it over. Appreciate it. Do little changes. See how you feel after doing those. That way you will maintain your unique face and can still feminize it as you see fit. You may find, for example, that a tracheal shave and a nose job are just fine for you, and decide to not do more.

Once again, do not become paranoid about your face. Do not pick apart every little piece of it. Women come in all shapes and sizes remember. Start looking at women's faces. They are usually not perfect! Why should yours have to be. You do not have to look like Barbie to be a beautiful, feminine woman.

Your face not being "perfect" does not make you any less of a woman. IN fact, it makes you more of one. Celebrate your unique face. It is part of what makes you, YOU!

Sex Reassignment Surgery (SRS or GRS)

Sex Reassignment Surgery or Gender Reassignment Surgery involves making changes to your outside body to appear as the opposite gender. Unfortunately, they cannot literally change your gender, but they can make your body appear on the outside as a females. That is why it is called Sex Reassignment Surgery rather than Sex Change surgery.

The surgery is obviously complex but essentially involves removing most of the tissue within the penis and then inverting the penis skin inward and creating a vagina.

Obviously, it can make you finally appear totally female on the outside. In many states you can legally change your gender to female (but this varies from state to state, depending on where you were born, so check with your state of birth). For some, they just would feel more complete and "totally female" on the outside.

This is an important area to learn about and give a lot of serious thought to. It can be a great thing, or a big mistake, so do not enter into it lightly as once it is done, it is done.

The important thing here is, as I have stressed many times in this book, is not to think of this as the be all and end all. It does not MAKE you a woman (although in many states you can then legally change your gender) – you already ARE a woman. It does not legitimize you – you already are legitimate. Remember, outside things do not make you a woman. It is what you have inside. No matter what anybody says. No matter what you do or have done to you. Do not look to the outside to make you feel better, as outside things will not make you happy in the long term.

Sex reassignment surgery is major surgery, obviously. There are many doctors out there who perform this, both in the US and abroad (especially in Thailand, where the surgery can be much cheaper). They all have their own methods and differences in results, so you will want to do some research on this yourself when you get to this point. Some give good "visual" results, but you lose feeling (which can be bad for sex). Some are very good in maintaining feeling, but it does not look as natural. And some are good at both (retaining feeling and looks), which is obviously what you are aiming for.

Your therapist can guide you on this. As surgeons change, and the best surgeon may change by the time you read this, I shall not recommend a particular surgeon. I would recommend talking this over with your therapist as you transition. It is not something you need to know an answer to until you have been transitioning for awhile. You may start out your transition wanting to have SRS and then change your mind along the way.

That is what happened with me. Once I was living full time for awhile and had gotten breast augmentation, I found I did not have as burning a desire to have SRS. I was already living and being treated as a woman, which is what mattered to me. To me, my penis was "just there". I really did not give it any more thought than I did my foot, so having SRS was not as important to me. This was my personal experience. Yours may be different. SRS is a personal decision.

Prior to have SRS, you will need to have done the following:

1) Lived full time as a female for at least one year.
2) Obtained two letters of recommendation from two separate therapists or psychiatrists after an appropriate amount of therapy.
3) Engage in hormone therapy for at least one year prior to surgery. This can be worked around with the right surgeon if you do not want to (e.g. if you do not like taking drugs) or cannot (as in my case after the blood clots) take hormones. I was going to go to Dr. Shrang

(who is retired now), and all I needed was a letter from a doctor stating why I could not take hormones. In my opinion, this hormone requirement needs to be changed. It can put people at risk health wise and is a personal choice. The first two requirements are very wise, however.

4) HIV test (usually)

Depending on your surgeon, you may also need to have hair removed "down there" around the area of penis so you will not have hair growing in your new vagina.

These "pre-requirements" are there for your protection, to ensure you do not do something you would regret later and are making a MAJOR change that is right for you. Do not be impatient with these requirements. They truly are there for your safety. I have talked to and read of girls who have had the surgery and regretted it. They wake up a year later and wonder why they have done that to their body, and they cannot go back now. They may have been hoping that would make them happy and find out it has not. Or they may have lost sexual feeling, and miss that. Or they may just find they were happier being preoperative and did not need the surgery to be happy after all.

This does not always happen. I have also talked to women who were very happy afterwards. Give yourself the time to really think about it and live your life full time to see if this is really the option that is right for you.

In the meantime, you can truly enjoy your transition. Remember, "Happiness Now!" You are being you. That is a real joy.

Girls have different reasons for wanting to have SRS. Let us go through some of these.

Here are some bad reasons to do it:

1) I can date men without telling them. You do not want to do something major like SRS for this reason. There are plenty of men who will like you pre-op and still treat you like a woman. And you are still going to have to tell them if you get serious, so there is still that issue.
2) To make you into a woman. You already are a woman. You do not need surgery for that.
3) To make you feel legitimate. Surgery is not going to help you there, as this is usually an internal struggle you are having that will still be there after surgery. You already are legitimate.
4) For sexual reasons. To catch men. Same reasoning as Number 1. This is a REALLY bad reason to have SRS.
5) Because you think you HAVE to do this. You do not have to do this to be a woman or to be a TS or to complete your transition. It is a personal choice.
6) You hate your penis. It is important to love every part of your body. It can be very feminine, believe it or not. But it is not bad to want to have a vagina instead. Just do not HATE what you have now as that may indicate a deeper issue inside.

Now here are some good reasons to do it:

1) You would feel more complete (but you are not looking for this to solve your problems or make you feel like a woman) as a woman.
2) Having a vagina seems very natural to you.

These are about it. If it just feels natural to you to have a vagina and you want to appear all female on the outside, then this may be the right choice for you. As long as you are not doing it to "fix" a problem or to fulfill you somehow.

I cannot make this decision for you. Only you can. I just do not want you to do it for the wrong reasons or to rush into it. Only you can decide if it is right for you.

If you have a burning desire to do it, and you just want to be "all woman" physically, and you are already comfortable with who you are and feel like a woman already, then go for it.

Once again, make sure you follow the pre-requirements prior to having SRS, even if you go overseas for the surgery. The requirements are there for your protection. The key requirements, once again, are as follows:

1) Two letters from two separate therapists who have evaluated you and recommend you for SRS.
2) Living full time as a woman for one year minimum.
3) Hormones for a year (be careful of these, as I've said)

I think the first two requirements are the keys. These will help you really determine if this is for you. After living full time, you may find living totally in the opposite gender is not for you. Maybe you will find you are happy just living full time and do not desire SRS anymore. But at the end of the year, you may be ready and know that SRS is right for you. So go for it.

Some other things to take into consideration:

1) Are you ready to live as a woman for the rest of your life. Woman are treated differently in this world. Some of the benefits you had as a man will be gone. However, being a woman is a great gift. Just keep this in mind.
2) Do you think you will miss your penis? Make sure of this. We get trained to hate it, and then after the surgery, you might not have much or any sensation down there or be able to orgasm. There are good surgeons who are better at ensuring you don't lose sensation, but this is still a risk.

3) Would you be ok if you lost feeling sexually after the surgery? This is a source of depression for some girls after the surgery, which is why I bring it up.

If you can answer yes to all these questions, then it's time to go.

I am not trying to discourage you from doing SRS. But I am trying to discourage you from doing it for the wrong reasons. I do not want anybody to wake up a year after surgery and wondering why they deformed their body (not that it is like this for most girls, unless you wish you had your penis back).

A therapist will really help you find the answer to this if you are confused. Remember, they are not gatekeepers. They are there to help you and support you.

Helpful Insights 5

1) Do NOT think of your transgenderism as a "condition" or as a "sickness" and avoid anybody (including other TS's) who refers to it as such.

These terms make it sound like there is something wrong with you. There is NOTHING wrong with you. You were made just perfect. It is no more a "condition" then being a man or being a woman is. This is just who you are and it is wonderful! It is a wonderful gift. You get to experience both genders in your life. You have a special sensitivity and understanding that genetic males and females do not have.

2) **You are not JUST a transsexual (or CD, TV, drag queen, etc)**

You are not just a transsexual. You are a human being. A human being with your own unique personality, hobbies, career, roles in life, friends, child, parent, spouse, etc.

Yes your gender is part of who you are, but it no more defines you as a person than a man is defined by being a man or a woman by being a woman. Your gender is just one aspect of the wonderful you.

3) **Develop a good sense of humor.**

This will carry you through anything. Do not take yourself too seriously. Learn to see the humor in things. This does not mean you do not respect yourself or love yourself or stick up for yourself or demean yourself. NO WAY. You respect yourself tremendously and you should never allow somebody to disrespect you! Just learn to lighten up a bit and enjoy life. It makes the journey (and life) more enjoyable!

4) **Do not forget to have fun.**

Everything about your transition is not serious. It is easy to get into this mindset, but do not forget to have fun with it too. Enjoy putting on makeup, learning to dress and walk, going out, etc. Your transition should be fun too!

5) **When working on passability, concentrate on the neck up first.**

The bulk of your passability will be associated with your face, hair and voice. So you want to work on those first. In other words, concentrate on removing facial hair, getting your makeup and hair right, training your voice, and doing any facial feminization surgery you want before doing anything like breast augmentation. Of course, if money is no object, you can do facial feminization surgery and breast augmentation at the same time. But make your face your first priority.

6) **"Pick your battles".**

What I mean by this is do not be ready to defend yourself every time somebody calls you "Sir' or "he" or makes a hurtful comment. Yes, it is disrespectful. Sometimes, though, they may not even realize they are doing anything wrong. Not everybody understands what a TS is. They may not have had any exposure to transgendered people or information about them, and may simply be ignorant.

However, sometimes it is best to just ignore it and say nothing unless you will be dealing with this person on a regular basis or they said something very offensive. Just shrug it off and move on with your life.

For example, if the grocery checkout clerk accidentally calls you "he", you might draw more attention to yourself saying "It's SHE" then by just ignoring it. However, if your sister or boss keeps calling you he long after you have gone full time, then you should correct them, or how will they learn? Just follow your gut. If something really bothers you and you feel the need to defend yourself, then say something. Just do not be constantly looking for a fight, or you will make yourself miserable. Once you start "picking your battles" and overlooking minor things more often, they happen less and less anyway, especially the further along you are in your transition.

Suggested Order of Transitioning

There is no one right order of steps to take, but here is a good order to follow as a starting point. Many of these steps would overlap, obviously, but this will at least give you an idea of what to concentrate on first. Steps 9 though 19 are more if you wish to transition to a full time female only, although you may still follow some of the "coming out" steps.

1) Go through the "What Brought you Here" section and make an initial decision on what you think you are and what you would like to do. Best guess. This can change. You might be a combination of some of the different types of transgendered people. But the key here is to give yourself a good starting point so you know what you need to do and what you do NOT need to do (or do not want to do). You do not have to make any big decisions on how far you want to go, if you want to go full time, make a career or relationship change, etc. In fact, do not worry about that yet.

2) Experiment with dressing. Buy some panties or a bra. Maybe even a dress if you are feeling brave. If you are living with someone, find a place to hide something special you can wear when you want.

3) If you feel sure about wanting to live as a woman or if you are comfortable removing hair permanently, find an electrologist or laser place and being removing hair. Start with your face first. If you have the money you can do other parts at the same time, but concentrate on the FACE first. Even if you choose to not go full time later or your desires change, it can never hurt to remove your beard. At least you will not have to shave, so no damage done.

4) If you are overweight, lose some weight. This is not meant critically or judgmentally, and if you are happy with yourself and how you look, then this is ok. Losing weight will help you to appear more feminine later, though and also you will need to be at a somewhat healthy weight for surgeries later, if you should so choose. Do not become bone skinny though. You still want to have a few curves. Just aim for a good healthy weight that you are comfortable with.

5) If you work out a lot and are bulked up, then stop building muscle. Switch to cardio, yoga, toning, stretching, Pilates etc. If you do not want or plan to live as a woman and do not care about passing and like being big and muscular, then of course skip this step. This is only if you want to look feminine and passable or really want to live as a female later.

6) Begin playing with makeup. This takes some practice. Have fun. Do not worry about being perfect. See the "Makeup" Section for tips.

7) Find a good wig to begin wearing at first. If you have a full head of hair and are comfortable doing that, you can start growing out your hair, even if just a little. See the "Hair" Section for more.

8) Find a therapist. This should be done as soon as possible if you are very confused or depressed or not sure where you want to go or are feeling very bad about yourself. See the "Therapy" Section.

9) Decide if you want to do hormones or not. ONLY do this step AFTER you have seen a therapist for at least two months and have a letter from them and ONLY under a qualified doctor's care. Only do this step if you feel it is

appropriate for you. ONLY do this step if you KNOW you are a woman inside and want to live as a woman. It is unwise and unneeded otherwise, as hormones are a serious step to take. See the "Hormones" section for more.

10) Decide if you want to do any facial feminization or body surgeries. Do you need to do any before going full time to be as passable as you like? If you feel yes, then start planning and scheduling those. Do NOT go overboard. Only do what is really necessary. Remember, appreciate the beauty of your face and you. Only do this if you want to live as a woman. See "Facial Feminization Surgery" for more.

11) Decide how to tell family, friends and work if you plan on going full time. See the "Coming Out" section.

12) Have a backup plan for work. You should be ok, but have a little savings or another job backup if you are not sure about your place of work.

13) Tell family and friends.

14) Tell Work.

15) Go Full Time (live full time as a female – at work, at home, everywhere) if you want to live as a woman now. If you do this and decide it is not for you (which does happen occasionally), remember you can always go back to living Part Time.

16) Get your name legally changed. See the "Your New Name" section.

17) Decide if you want SRS. If so, get a second therapist's letter. Be sure this is right for you. You have to live full

time as a woman for AT LEAST a year prior to doing this. I would recommend living full time at least a year prior to making this decision. You may find you do not feel the need for SRS. You do not need surgery to BE a woman. You already are.

18) If SRS is right for you (work with your therapist and do soul searching), then find an appropriate surgeon and make an appointment.

19) Enjoy your life! Do this throughout the journey! Do not forget everything else happening in your life either – job, friends, family, hobbies, etc. It is all part of the adventure!

Conclusion

Here we are at the end of the book already. I hope you have enjoyed reading this. I would suggest going back and reading it again, but in any case, keep this book as a guidebook, a reference manual, and companion to you throughout your transition. I hope this book can act as a friend and mentor to you throughout your transition.

When I got the idea for this book, I wanted transgendered women everywhere to finally have a practical guide that was nuts and bolts that they could follow and have a successful and happy transition to being the person they wanted to be – whether that was a full time woman, a part time crossdresser, or simply a feminine man who learned to love his female side. I wanted this book to also helped them achieve a more positive and balanced mindset and to learn to really love who they are.

I would just like to end with some encouraging words and final advice for your transition.

Learn to accept and LOVE who you are in this transition. Not just your gender, but all of you! The unique you.

Also, remember, you do not have to be like every other transgendered woman out there either. You be who YOU want to be, and do what YOU want to do.

You are a very special person. I believe you were made transgendered for a reason, and the world needs you!

As a transgendered woman, I believe you have a special kind of sensitivity and understanding that men and women do not have, as you have had to live in both genders.

You also have a special kind of courage, whether you know it or not. It takes guts to even buy a book like this and start to explore something you have had to hide your whole life. You do have the courage to do anything you want. This transition will show you that!

If you ever get scared along the way or do not feel comfortable doing something yet, do not do it. That is the beauty of this. This is YOUR life. You can do as little or as much as you want. That uncomfortable feeling might be telling you something is not right for you or that you are not ready for that yet. Just remember, though, sometimes we have to push ourselves a little to get over a bump.

Do not hurry anything too much as you go along. Enjoy your transition and enjoy your life. Everything will happen in the exact right time. Do not hurry into anything serious you have not thought through and know is right for you. Once again, it will all happen in the exact right time. And if you ever feel stressed or the need to get to a certain step to be happy, just remember the phrase "Happiness Now!!!!" and everything will be ok. That is a very calming thing to say by the way: "Everything will be ok". Try saying that one too very calmly, and you will be amazed how the stress will ease.

Remember, you have a right to be you. To pursue your dreams. You can do this all and still live a healthy, balanced, joyful life. Listen to the insights in this book and follow the steps, and you will have a positive transition.

Yes there are bumps along the way. Yes there are challenges. Yes there are scary things. But when you get to the other side – even if that is just dressing occasionally – it is worth all of it. You get to be you now!!!! You do not have to wish for that anymore.

YOU ARE BEING YOU!!!!!!!

Trust me, there is NOTHING better than that feeling!

Made in the USA
San Bernardino, CA
17 May 2014